AF416705

# Dancing With Donnie

## The Ballroom Awaits

Barry Robbins

# Copyright and Disclaimer

**Copyright © 2025 by Barry Robbins**

All rights reserved. No part of this book may be reproduced, stored in a retrieval system, or transmitted in any form or by any means, electronic, mechanical, photocopying, recording, or otherwise, without the prior written permission of the author, except in the case of brief quotations embodied in critical reviews and certain other noncommercial uses permitted by copyright law.

## DISCLAIMER

This is a work of satire and political commentary. While this book references real public figures and actual events (including President Donald Trump's July 31, 2025 announcement of plans for a White House ballroom), the audition process, dance sequences, and related events depicted herein are entirely fictional and products of the author's imagination.

No actual ballroom auditions occurred. No dance partners were selected. No dogs were harmed (or shot) in the writing of this book.

The portrayal of public figures in this work is satirical in nature and should not be interpreted as factual representation of their actual beliefs, actions, statements, or dance abilities. Any dialogue, thoughts, or actions attributed to real persons are fictional and created for satirical and comedic purposes.

This book is protected under the First Amendment of the United States Constitution as political satire and parody. The author does not claim that any events depicted actually occurred, nor does he assert any factual claims about the individuals portrayed.

If President Sheinbaum wishes to discuss this book, the author is available for conversation. All other parties seeking legal recours eare respectfully directed to their sense of humor.

## A Note on Satire

Satire has a long and venerable tradition in American letters and political discourse. From Mark Twain to Jonathan Swift, from Saturday Night Live to The Onion, humor has always been a vital tool for examining power, exposing absurdity, and speaking truth through exaggeration.

This book falls squarely in that tradition. It is not journalism. It is not biography. It is not a documentary record. It is satire—a comedic exploration of character, ego, and what happens when the absurd becomes reality.

If any resemblance to actual persons, living or dead (or dancing), causes offense, the author suggests they consider why satirical fiction strikes such a chord.



**Author's Note:**

No Yorkies, Terriers, or any other dogs were harmed in the creation of this work. The author is a dog lover and would never condone violence against our canine companions. Unlike certain characters depicted herein.

The author does, however, maintain that Rex the plastic dinosaur is one of the great philosophers of our time.

# Dedication

This book is dedicated to Pam, my caregiver extraordinaire, without whom this book would not be possible.

# Contents

# THE PROJECT

# Chapter 1
# The Announcement

**Part 1: Truth Social Post**

*Posted at 2:47 AM*

BIG ANNOUNCEMENT!!! After months of planning (actually years of thinking about this), I am building the most SPECTACULAR ballroom at the White House. $300 MILLION of the most beautiful construction you've ever seen. NOT ONE PENNY of taxpayer money - I'm paying for it myself along with some rich buddies because that's what real leaders do!!!

90,000 square feet of pure MAGNIFICENCE. Italian marble floors (the best marble, I know the quarry owner personally), Austrian crystal chandeliers (bigger than Versailles!), gold everything. REAL GOLD, not painted fake gold like other people use. The East Wing is GONE - nobody even knew what it was for anyway!

For 150 YEARS presidents have wanted a proper ballroom and FAILED. I'm the only one with the vision and the SKILL to make it happen. I am probably the best ballroom builder in the history of the world, maybe ever. When foreign leaders see this they will be AMAZED at what America can do under the right leadership!!!

The fake news will say "Trump is wasting money" but they're WRONG as usual. This is an INVESTMENT in America's future. Every future president will thank me. They'll say "Thank you President Trump for having the COURAGE to build something truly great."

Construction starts IMMEDIATELY. The best contractors (I know all the best contractors), the finest materials, completed before the end of my term. We're talking about the most incredible grand opening in White House history. Maybe in world history!

The haters and losers will complain but they always do. They complained about Trump Tower, they complained about Mar-a-Lago, they complained about everything beautiful I've ever built. But then they see the results and they say "WOW, how did he do it?"

This ballroom will be used for STATE DINNERS (no more terrible tents in the rain!), business summits with the world's most successful people, and celebrations that the whole world will watch.

I have been thinking about this for a LONG TIME. When I see those pathetic tents on the South Lawn and watch beautiful women in evening gowns getting soaked and muddy walking to dinner, I think "This is not the America I want to lead." America deserves BETTER. America deserves TRUMP QUALITY.

The timing is perfect. The American people are ready for something SPECTACULAR. Something that shows the world we are the greatest nation on earth and we have the greatest leader in our history!

More details coming soon. This is going to be INCREDIBLE!

#MAGA  #BallroomTime  #TrumpQuality  #WhiteHouse #MakeAmericaDanceAgain

## Part 2: Press Briefing with Karoline Leavitt

*The following afternoon*

**LEAVITT:** Good afternoon, everyone. I'd like to address the President's announcement regarding the White House ballroom project, and then I'll take your questions.

As the President outlined in his social media post, this exciting initiative will address a longstanding infrastructure need at the White House. For over a century and a half, presidents and their staffs have recognized the limitations of current event space, which often requires temporary, weather-dependent solutions.

The proposed 90,000-square-foot ballroom facility will provide a permanent, climate-controlled venue for state dinners, diplomatic receptions, and other official functions. The project will be entirely privately funded through the President and his donors, with no impact on the federal budget.

Construction is targeted to begin this September, with completion scheduled for January 2029. The President will be personally involved in the design and oversight process, drawing on his extensive background in construction and development.

Yes, Peter?

**REPORTER:** Karoline, can you clarify what happens to the East Wing staff when construction begins?

**LEAVITT:** The administration is working on transition plans for affected personnel. We're committed to ensuring continuity of operations throughout the construction process.

**REPORTER:** Has the Committee for the Preservation of the White House signed off on removing the East Wing entirely?

**LEAVITT:** We're working with all relevant oversight bodies to ensure proper procedures are followed. Next question.

**REPORTER:** The President said he's "probably the best ball-room builder in the history of the world." Can you elaborate on his specific ballroom construction experience?

**LEAVITT:** The President has decades of experience in luxury real estate development, including venues that host large-scale events. His properties regularly accommodate sophisticated gatherings that require the same attention to acoustics, lighting, and spatial design that this project demands.

**REPORTER:** Will there be public tours of the new ballroom?

**LEAVITT:** Those operational details are still being finalized.

**REPORTER:** Karoline, does the President actually know how to dance?

**LEAVITT:** I'm sorry, what?

**REPORTER:** Well, he's building a ballroom. Does he dance?

**LEAVITT:** The ballroom will serve multiple functions beyond dancing. State dinners, receptions, diplomatic meetings—

**REPORTER:** But specifically, can the President dance?

**LEAVITT:** I haven't discussed the President's recreational activities with him in that level of detail.

**REPORTER:** Has the President taken dance lessons in preparation for using the ballroom?

**LEAVITT:** I think we're getting a bit off track here. The ballroom is a serious infrastructure improvement that will benefit this and future administrations.

**REPORTER:** But surely if you're building a ballroom, dancing is relevant?

**LEAVITT:** The President is naturally gifted at many things. I'm confident he'll rise to any occasion. Next question—about the ballroom project specifically, please.

**REPORTER:** What style of ballroom dancing does the President prefer?

**LEAVITT:** [Long pause] I'll... I'll follow up with you on that.

# Part 3: Trump Press Conference

*Two days later, Rose Garden*

**TRUMP:** Thank you, thank you everyone. Beautiful day, isn't it? Perfect day to talk about something beautiful—the most incredible ballroom project in the history of ballrooms.

I've been getting tremendous response to this announcement. Tremendous. World leaders calling to congratulate me on my vision. Business leaders saying they've never seen anything like it. Even some Democrats—not many, but some—admitting this is a fantastic idea.

You know, I was just talking to someone—very important person, won't say who—and they said, "Sir, how did you think of something so brilliant?" And I told them, it's natural. It's instinct. When you're a great builder, when you understand luxury like I understand luxury, these ideas just come to you.

**REPORTER:** Mr. President, critics are saying this is an expensive distraction from more pressing issues—

**TRUMP:** Fake news. Fake, fake, fake. This isn't expensive, it's an investment. A tremendous investment in America's prestige. And pressing issues? I've solved more pressing issues than any president in history. Probably more than Lincoln and Washington combined.

**REPORTER:** Sir, can you tell us about your own dancing experience?

**TRUMP:** My dancing? [chuckles] Oh, I'm a very good dancer. Very, very good. People don't know this about me, but I'm probably the best dancing president we've ever had. Better than Obama, much better than Biden—though that's not saying much.

**REPORTER:** Could you show us some moves?

**TRUMP:** Show you? [steps away from podium] You want me to show you?

**SECRET SERVICE AGENT:** [stepping forward] Sir, maybe we should—

**TRUMP:** No, no, it's fine. People should see what real talent looks like.

[Trump begins what appears to be his interpretation of a box step, arms awkwardly positioned, taking small, careful steps]

**TRUMP:** This is a waltz. Very sophisticated dance. Most people can't do this properly, but I have natural rhythm. [continues stepping, slightly off-balance] You see how smooth that is? That's years of natural ability.

**REPORTER:** Mr. President, you seem to be—

**TRUMP:** [attempting a turn, nearly tripping] That's an advanced move right there. Very advanced. [steadying himself on the podium] The ballroom will have much better floors for this kind of thing. These flagstones are terrible for dancing. Terrible!

[His tie has twisted around, jacket slightly askew]

**TRUMP:** Now, the foxtrot—[takes a step backward, microphone cord catching his foot]—this is even more sophisticated. [stumbling slightly] You have to have tremendous balance for the foxtrot. Tremendous.

**REPORTER:** Sir, are you okay?

**TRUMP:** [straightening his jacket] Perfect. I'm perfect. That was just a preview of what you'll see at the grand opening. Much better with the right partner, of course. I'll need someone who can keep up with my skill level.

**REPORTER:** Have you selected a dance partner for the opening?

**TRUMP:** [freezing mid-step] A dance partner?

**REPORTER:** For the first dance in the new ballroom.

**TRUMP:** [long pause, looking suddenly uncertain] Well, obviously... obviously I'll need... that is, there will be...

[Another long pause as the reality seems to hit him]

**TRUMP:** [recovering quickly] That's going to be a tremendous surprise. A fantastic surprise. Someone very special. Someone who appreciates real dancing talent when they see it.

**REPORTER:** But you haven't chosen anyone yet?

**TRUMP:** [straightening his tie nervously] The selection process will be... very thorough. Very professional. Only the best for the most beautiful ballroom in the world.

[Walks quickly back toward the White House]

**TRUMP:** [over his shoulder] No more questions about dancing! Ask me about the marble! Ask me about the chandeliers!

# Chapter 2
# The Preparation

The dance instructor arrived at the White House at 11 PM on a Tuesday, escorted through a side entrance normally used for classified briefings. She'd been told to bring no identification, tell no one where she was going, and sign a non-disclosure agreement so comprehensive it covered not just what she saw but what she heard, smelled, and potentially thought about.

"This is very irregular," Madame Olga Konstantinova said as a Secret Service agent guided her through dimmed hallways.

"The President values discretion."

"The President wants dance lessons at eleven at night?"

"The President wants many things. Dancing is relatively normal."

They arrived at the East Room. Donald Trump stood in the center of the parquet floor, wearing a tuxedo that looked like it had been purchased that afternoon and already regretted.

"You're the dance teacher?"

"I am Madame Konstantinova. I have taught—"

"Great, great. Let's get started. And remember—" He pointed at her with both index fingers. "This never happened. You were never here. I already know how to dance. This is just a... a refinement session."

"Of course, Mr. President."

"I'm naturally very good. Probably the best natural dancer you've ever seen. But my advisors—idiots, by the way—suggested I might want to brush up on some technical details. Minor details. Details that don't even matter."

Madame Konstantinova had taught oligarchs, oil barons, and a Saudi prince who'd threatened to behead her for correcting his posture. She was unflappable.

"Shall we begin with your stance?"

"My stance is perfect."

"Of course. But perhaps we could make it more... perfectly perfect?"

Trump considered this. "Fine. Show me."

She demonstrated proper ballroom posture—shoulders back, core engaged, weight balanced. Trump attempted to mirror her, immediately leaning forward from the hips.

"You're tilting, Mr. President."

"I'm not tilting. This is power posture. Very commanding."

"For business, perhaps. For dancing, you need to be vertical."

"I AM vertical!"

Madame Konstantinova produced a small level from her bag and held it against his back. The bubble was nowhere near center.

Trump stared at it. "That level is broken."

"Sir—"

"BROKEN. Get a new level. A better level. An American level, not some Russian—are you Russian?"

"I am from Brighton Beach. By way of Moscow. By way of—"

"Never mind. Just show me the steps."

They began with a basic box step. Trump counted out loud—"ONE-two-three, ONE-two-three"—emphasizing the first beat with such force that he nearly stomped through the floor.

"Lighter, Mr. President. Like a cat."

"Cats don't waltz."

"Metaphorically. You should be light on your feet."

"I weigh 215 pounds. Very muscular. I can't be light."

"Then be... less heavy."

"That doesn't make sense."

They continued. Trump's arms stuck out at odd angles, his frame collapsed every third step, and he kept trying to lead even though Madame Konstantinova was leading.

"You must allow yourself to be guided," she said.

"I don't get guided. I do the guiding. That's my thing."

"In ballroom dancing—"

"I'll lead. You follow. That's how it works."

"But sir, I am teaching you to lead by showing you what leading feels like—"

"Sounds like communism."

By midnight, they'd managed three consecutive box steps without Trump either tilting, stomping, or arguing about the fundamental nature of leading. Madame Konstantinova considered it a victory.

"Same time tomorrow?" Trump asked.

"You want more lessons?"

"These aren't lessons. These are consultations. Big difference. And yes. Every night this week. But remember—"

"This never happened."

"Exactly. You're a smart lady. For a Russian."

"Thank you, Mr. President. That is... thank you."


Three days later, Trump summoned his Chief of Staff to the White House theater.

"I need the kitchen staff. All of them."

"Sir?"

"The kitchen staff. The people who cook. Bring them here."

"May I ask why?"

"Research. For the ballroom project. Very important research."

Twenty minutes later, eight confused kitchen workers sat in the theater while Trump stood before a massive screen, remote control in hand.

"Thank you all for coming," Trump said. "What we're about to do is classified. Top secret. If anyone asks, this meeting never happened."

The head chef raised his hand. "Sir, we're watching a movie?"

"Not just any movie. The greatest dance movies ever made. I'm studying the masters. Learning their techniques. You're going to help me."

He pressed play. The screen filled with Fred Astaire and Ginger Rogers in "Top Hat."

For twenty minutes, they watched in silence as Astaire glided across the screen with impossible grace. Then Trump paused it.

"See that? That's what I'm going for. That smooth thing he does."

"Mr. President," the pastry chef said carefully, "Fred Astaire trained for decades—"

"I can do that. I have natural rhythm. I just need to see it a few times."

He rewound, watched again, then stood up. "You—" He pointed at the sous chef, a small woman from Guatemala. "Stand up. We're doing the lift."

"The... what?"

"The lift. Like Astaire. Come here."

"Sir, I don't think—"

"It's fine. I'm very strong. Strongest president ever. Probably stronger than Teddy Roosevelt."

The sous chef stood reluctantly. Trump positioned himself behind her, grabbed her waist, and attempted to lift her as Astaire had lifted Rogers.

He managed to raise her approximately four inches before his back made an alarming sound.

"SIR!"

Trump released her, stumbling backward. "The floor is uneven. That's the problem. The floor."

"Should we call the doctor?" the head chef asked.

"No! I'm fine. Perfectly fine. Very limber. We're just going to focus on the non-lifting parts."

They watched Gene Kelly in "Singin' in the Rain." Trump tried to replicate the umbrella twirling. He broke two umbrellas and nearly took out a lighting fixture.

They watched "Shall We Dance." Trump attempted to spin like Astaire. He got dizzy after one rotation and sat down heavily.

"Why does he make it look so easy?" Trump muttered.

"Practice, sir," the head chef offered. "Decades of practice."

"I don't have decades. I have four years. Less than four years. We need to speed this up."

He fast-forwarded through the romantic parts—"Boring, very boring"—and paused on the dance sequences, studying them frame by frame.

"Rita Hayworth," he said as "Gilda" began. "Very beautiful woman. Great dancer. You—" He pointed at the line cook, a young man from Honduras. "You're Rita now."

"Sir?"

"Stand up. We're doing the glove thing."

"The... I don't have gloves, sir."

"Improvise. Use oven mitts."

What followed was Trump attempting to recreate Rita Hayworth's sultry glove removal while his "Rita" stood holding oven mitts, looking like he wanted to be anywhere else.

"More passion!" Trump commanded. "Rita had passion!"

"Sir, I make empanadas."

"Now you make MAGIC. Do it again!"

By 2 AM, they'd watched seven films, broken three props, and Trump had attempted to dance with five different members of the kitchen staff. The head chef had been dipped (unsuccessfully), the pastry chef had been spun (nearly into the wall), and the dishwasher had been enlisted as "backup Astaire" for reasons no one quite understood.

"Same time tomorrow," Trump announced as he dismissed them. "And remember—this is classified. Top secret. Kitchen-staff-eyes-only."

They filed out in stunned silence.

"Did that just happen?" the sous chef whispered.

"I think so," the head chef replied. "But I also think we all signed NDAs, so let's never speak of it again."

"Deal."


The lessons and movie sessions continued for two weeks. Madame Konstantinova managed to teach Trump approximately one and a half competent dance moves. The kitchen staff learned that Gene Kelly made everything look easier than it was, and that the President could not, under any circumstances, be lifted over anyone's head, nor could he lift anyone over his.

On the final night, Trump stood in the East Room, attempting what Madame Konstantinova had dubbed "the presidential waltz"—a simplified version of a waltz that involved minimal turning, no dipping, and constant counting out loud.

"ONE-two-three, ONE-two-three," Trump counted, moving through the steps with the sous chef, who'd been volunteered as his final practice partner.

"Better, Mr. President," Madame Konstantinova said. "Much better."

"I'm a natural. I told you."

"Yes, sir. Very natural."

"I'm ready for the real thing now. Ready for my dance partner. Whoever she is, she's going to be very impressed."

Madame Konstantinova and the sous chef exchanged glances.

"We shall see, Mr. President," Madame Konstantinova said diplomatically. "We shall see."

After Trump left, she turned to the sous chef. "That man is going to humiliate himself."

"Should we warn someone?"

"Who would we warn? And who would believe us?" She packed her things. "Besides, we were never here. This never happened."

"Right. Never happened."

They left through the side entrance, taking with them the knowledge that the President of the United States had spent two weeks trying to learn to dance and had achieved a skill level best described as "ambitious kindergartener."

The sous chef paused at the door. "Do you think he'll actually find someone to dance with?"

Madame Konstantinova smiled grimly. "I think someone will find him. And I think it will be spectacular."

"Good spectacular or bad spectacular?"

"In my experience," Madame Konstantinova said, pulling her coat tight against the November cold, "with men like him, there is no difference."

# Chapter 3

# The Search

The phone call came three weeks after Trump's Rose Garden dance demonstration went viral. Michelle Obama was in her home office, reviewing speaking invitations, when her assistant buzzed.

"Mrs. Obama, the White House Chief of Staff is on line one."

Michelle set down her pen. "Which White House?"

"The current one."

"I'll take it."

She picked up, already regretting it. "This is Michelle Obama."

"Mrs. Obama, thank you for taking my call. I'm calling on behalf of President Trump regarding a matter of some... delicacy."

"Go on."

"As you may have seen, the President has announced plans for a ballroom addition to the White House—"

"I saw the announcement. I also saw him fall over trying to demonstrate a waltz."

A pause. "Yes. That was... unfortunate."

"That was hilarious."

"Be that as it may, the President has decided that the selection of his dance partner for the inaugural event should be a formal process. We'd like you to oversee it."

Michelle leaned back in her chair, intrigued despite herself. "Why me?"

"Because it would lend credibility to the process. And we'd like you to serve as the judge."

"Why on earth would I do that?"

"Because it would be an opportunity to ensure the process maintains dignity and—"

"There is no version of this that maintains dignity."

"Nevertheless, your involvement would lend the process credibility. And perhaps ensure the President selects someone... appropriate."

Michelle was quiet for a long moment, her mind already three steps ahead. The opportunity for chaos. The chance to watch Trump squirm through auditions. The possibility of selecting someone who would humble him on the world stage.

"I'll need complete authority," she said. "No interference from the President or his staff."

"Of course."

"I select the final partner. My decision is binding."

"Agreed."

"And I want it in writing."

"We'll have a formal agreement drawn up by tomorrow."

After she hung up, Barack appeared in the doorway. "Did I just hear you agree to help Trump find a dance partner?"

"You did."

"Why?"

Michelle smiled. "Because I'm going to enjoy this more than anything I've done since leaving the White House."

"That sounds ominous."

"That sounds like justice."

The official announcement came two days later. Michelle Obama, former First Lady, would serve as the sole judge for the President's Dance Partner Selection Process. Applications would be accepted from anyone, anywhere in the world, for a period of three weeks.

The announcement itself was a study in contrasts—Michelle's team had written it, and it showed.

## OFFICIAL ANNOUNCEMENT Office of the Former First Lady

Mrs. Michelle Obama has agreed to serve as the independent selector for President Trump's dance partner for the inaugural White House Grand Ballroom event.

The selection process will be open to any interested individual who meets the following criteria:

• Must be 18 years of age or older (exceptions granted on a case-by-case basis)
• Must be able to travel to Washington, D.C. for an in-person audition
• Must have basic ballroom dancing ability (or be willing to learn)
• Must be available for the inaugural event in January 2029

## Application Requirements:

Submit the following materials to WhiteHouseDanceAuditions @obama.org:

1. Full name and contact information

2. Brief biography (maximum 200 words)

3. Essay: "Why I Should Dance With President Trump" (maximum 100 words)

4. Confirmation of availability for in-person audition in Washington, D.C.

Applications will be accepted from November 1, 2025 through November 21, 2025.

Mrs. Obama will personally review all applications and select candidates for in-person auditions. Her selection of the final dance partner will be binding and final.

This is a voluntary position. No compensation will be provided.

The response was immediate and overwhelming.

By the end of the first day, Michelle's team had received 1,247 applications. By the end of the first week, over 15,000. By the time the application period closed, the final count was 23,691 applications from 147 countries.

Michelle sat in her office with her assistant, scrolling through the flood of submissions.

"This is insane," her assistant said. "How are we going to review twenty-three thousand applications?"

"We're not. We're going to review the interesting ones." Michelle pulled up a random application. "Let's see what we're working with."

She clicked on the first essay.

## Application #1: Brad from Scottsdale, Arizona

*Why I Should Dance With President Trump:*

bro i saw him dancing in the rose garden and i was like omg i could totally do better than that. ive been watching dance moms with my girlfriend for like 3 years so i basically know all the moves. also i think it would be super cool to be on tv and maybe get some instagram followers out of it? my buddy steve says trump cant dance for shit but i think if he had a good partner (me) he could probably be ok. also i need a job lol.

Michelle looked at her assistant. "That's a no."
"Obviously."
She clicked to the next one.

## Application #2: Maria Sánchez from Madrid, Spain

*Why I Should Dance With President Trump:*

I have been a professional ballroom dancer for twenty-three years, with championships in both International Standard and Latin categories. I believe this presents a unique opportunity to represent Spain on the world stage and to demonstrate the true artistry of ballroom dance. While I understand President Trump is still developing his technique, I am confident that with proper guidance and professional partnership, we could create a memorable performance. I approach this with the utmost seriousness and respect for the art form.

"Now that's interesting," Michelle said. "She thinks this is a real competition."

"Should we tell her it's not?"

"Absolutely not. Put her in the maybe pile."

Michelle continued scrolling, stopping on particularly notable submissions.

## Application #3: Dorothy Henderson from Topeka, Kansas

*Why I Should Dance With President Trump:*

My grandson showed me the announcement and said I should apply as a joke, but I don't think it's a joke at all! I've been dancing since I was a little girl, and I think it would be just wonderful to dance with a President. My late husband Harold and I used to go dancing every Saturday night at the Elks Lodge, and everyone said we were the best dancers in Topeka. I know President Trump is very busy with important President things, but I promise I'm a very good dancer and I won't step on his feet too much. It would be the thrill of my lifetime!

"Oh my god," Michelle's assistant said. "She's sincere."

"Completely sincere. She has no idea what she's walking into." Michelle made a note.

"Definitely interviewing her. This could be amazing."

## Application #4: Dmitri Volkov from San Francisco, California

*Why I Should Dance With President Trump:*

Traditional ballroom dancing is fundamentally broken. The hierarchical lead-follow dynamic reinforces outdated power structures. I'm disrupting the space with my platform, DanceChain—a blockchain-based approach to partner dancing that democratizes movement and creates value through tokenized choreography. Dancing with Trump would be the ultimate proof of concept. We're pre-Series A but have strong VC interest. Also, I took a salsa class once.

Michelle stared at the screen. "Is this real?"
"Silicon Valley is a hellscape."
"Put him in the yes pile. I need to see this in person."

## Application #5: Tyler Morrison from Indianapolis, Indiana

*Why I Should Dance With President Trump:*

my girlfriend dared me to apply and said if i didnt she would break up with me. so here i am. i dont really want to dance with trump. i dont even like dancing. i just want to keep my girlfriend. please dont pick me. but if you do pick me i guess i have to do it because i already told everyone i applied and now i cant back out. this sucks.

"The girlfriend is evil," her assistant observed.
"The girlfriend is a genius. Yes pile."

## Application #6: Brandi Kowalski from Boca Raton, Florida

*Why I Should Dance With President Trump:*

I have been in love with Donald Trump since I first saw him on The Apprentice. He is the most handsome, intelligent, powerful man in the world and it would be my absolute DREAM to dance with him. I have taken three ballroom classes and I know we would have AMAZING chemistry. I am also available for dating after the dance if he is interested (I know he's married but Melania seems cold and I am very warm and affectionate). I have attached several photos of myself in evening gowns. Please consider me. I would make him SO happy. We are MEANT TO BE TOGETHER.

"That's a restraining order waiting to happen," Michelle's assistant said.

"That's also going in the yes pile. I want to see his face when he reads this."

"You're cruel."

"I'm thorough."

## Application #7: Svetlana Novak from Prague, Czech Republic

*Why I Should Dance With President Trump:*

I grew up in Czechoslovakia under communism. We had to dance with many people we did not like. It was required. This is same, but with better lighting and probably worse dancing. I am professional ballroom instructor. I have seen everything. I have taught oligarchs who threatened to kill me for correcting posture. I have taught drunk businessmen who think they are Fred Astaire. Trump cannot be worse. (Probably.) If you select me, I will be professional, competent, and only slightly sarcastic. This is best offer you will receive.

"I love her," Michelle said. "Yes pile immediately."

## Application #8: Marcus Turner from Atlanta, Georgia

*Why I Should Dance With President Trump:*

I am NOT applying because I want to dance with this man. I am applying because someone needs to tell him to his FACE what a disaster he has been for this country. Dancing with him gives me three minutes of his attention where he CAN'T walk away or tweet insults. Three minutes to tell him about the families separated at the border. The healthcare he tried to destroy. The climate crisis he ignored. The pandemic he mishandled. If you pick me, I WILL dance with him. But I will also make sure he hears EVERY SINGLE TRUTH he's been avoiding. He owes this country answers. I'll get them during the waltz.

Michelle's assistant looked concerned. "That seems like it could get... confrontational."
"That seems like it could get interesting. Yes pile."

## Application #9: Tiffany Chen from Los Angeles, California

*Why I Should Dance With President Trump:*

Is this for a new season of Dancing with the Stars? I've been trying to get on DWTS for YEARS and this seems like a backdoor way in! I have 2.3 million TikTok followers and I do dance content so I'm like, super qualified? I know Trump was on The Apprentice so he obviously understands reality TV. We could make this

HUGE. I'm thinking we do like a whole journey arc where I teach him to dance and we have ups and downs but ultimately triumph together? Very emotional, very viral. My agent says this could be my big break. When do we start filming?

"She thinks this is reality TV," Michelle said.
"Should we tell her it's not?"
"Where's the fun in that? Yes pile."

Michelle leaned back, scrolling through hundreds more applications. Love letters from supporters. Angry screeds from critics. Earnest submissions from professional dancers. Joke applications from teenagers. Marriage proposals. Death threats. A surprising number of people who thought this was a reality TV show casting call.

"This is going to be chaos," her assistant said.

"This is going to be perfect," Michelle corrected. "Start scheduling auditions. I want to see at least twenty candidates. Maybe more."

"What are we looking for?"

Michelle smiled. "Maximum entertainment value. And maybe, if we're lucky, someone who will make Donald Trump profoundly uncomfortable on national television."

"That's not very professional."

"No," Michelle agreed. "But it's going to be incredibly satisfying."

She pulled up the master list and began marking names. Politicians. World leaders. Celebrities. Complete unknowns. Each one representing a different flavor of chaos.

By the time she finished, she had a list of twenty candidates who would be invited to audition.

Not one of them was what Donald Trump expected.

Which was exactly the point.

# THE AUDITIONS

# Chapter 4

# The First Audition

Michelle Obama arrived at the White House at 9 AM on a cold December morning. Secret Service escorted her through the main entrance. The East Wing was gone—completely demolished. Where Jacqueline Kennedy's office had once stood, there was now rubble, construction equipment, and an enormous pit that would eventually become Trump's ballroom.

"We've set up the East Room for the auditions," her escort said. "The President specifically requested the largest room in the White House."

"Of course he did."

The East Room—scene of Theodore Roosevelt's children's roller-skating parties, site of seven presidential funeral services, location of countless state receptions—had been transformed. A Steinway grand piano sat in the corner near the windows overlooking the North Lawn. A professional accompanist was already warming up. A small table held Michelle's materials—notepads, pens, water. Three chairs had been arranged in the space: one for her, one for Trump, one for the candidate.

Trump wasn't there yet.

Michelle walked across the parquet floor, her footsteps echoing in the cavernous room. Twenty-eight feet high ceilings. Nearly three thousand square feet of space. Gold damask draperies framing six-foot windows. Gilbert Stuart's portrait of George Washington watching from the wall—the same portrait Dolley Madison had saved when the British burned the White House in 1814.

And now: ballroom dance auditions.

She opened her notebook to the first page. Twenty names. Twenty auditions scheduled over the next several weeks. She'd arranged them carefully—some for maximum chaos, some for genuine curiosity, all for reasons Trump would never understand.

Vladimir Putin was first.

When Trump's Chief of Staff had seen the schedule, she'd called immediately. "Mrs. Obama, are you sure about starting with President Putin?"

"Completely sure."

"The optics—"

"Are exactly what they should be. If the President wants a spectacle, he'll get one."

The door opened. Trump entered, already in a tuxedo despite the 10:00 AM start time. His hair was freshly styled, his tie perfectly centered. He was trying very hard to look casual and failing completely.

"Michelle! You're here! Early! That's good, very professional."

"Mr. President."

"So." He looked around nervously at the vast room. "This is happening. The auditions. My dance partner selection. Very exciting. Historic, really. Probably the most watched dance auditions in history."

"Very likely."

"And you have someone coming this morning? Someone good?"

"Someone interesting."

"Interesting good or interesting bad?"

"Just interesting."

Trump's eyes narrowed. "You're not going to make this easy, are you?"

"Mr. President, you're building a three-hundred-million-dollar ballroom and you've invited the world to watch you select a dance partner. Nothing about this was ever going to be easy."

He opened his mouth to respond, then thought better of it. Instead, he took his seat, crossed his legs, uncrossed them, adjusted his jacket, and tried to look presidential.

The pianist continued warming up. Scales and arpeggios filled the enormous room.

Michelle reviewed her notes one more time. She'd written a single sentence at the top of the page, a reminder of why she was doing this:

*Let him show the world exactly who he is.*

At 10:00 AM precisely, the door opened again. A Secret Service agent stepped in.

"Madam, the first candidate has arrived."

Michelle looked up. "Send him in."

Trump leaned forward. "Who is it? You didn't tell me who's first."

"You'll see."

"Michelle, I'm the President. I should know—"

The door opened wide.

Vladimir Putin stepped into the East Room.

Trump's face went through several expressions in rapid succession: surprise, confusion, delight, and something that might have been nervousness.

"Vladimir!"

Putin surveyed the room with those calculating eyes, taking in the piano, the setup, Michelle's carefully neutral expression, Trump's barely contained excitement, and George Washington's portrait watching from the wall.

"Donald," Putin said. Then, to Michelle: "Mrs. Obama. Thank you for this... opportunity."

"Mr. President." Michelle gestured to the center of the room. "Shall we begin?"

Trump stood quickly, too quickly, nearly knocking over his chair. He straightened his jacket, smoothed his hair, and took three steps toward Putin before remembering he was supposed to wait for instruction.

Michelle opened her notebook.

The pianist's hands hovered over the keys.

And the auditions began.

# Chapter 5
# Vladimir Putin's Audition

Michelle had requested that only Putin's translator be present—a severe woman in her sixties who stood against the wall like a piece of furniture.

Putin moved to the center of the East Room with the economy of a predator. Behind him, two security men took positions by the door.

Trump was already moving forward, hand extended. "Vladimir! I'm so glad you could make it!"

Putin let him approach, then accepted the handshake with a grip that made Trump wince slightly.

"Donald," Putin said in accented English. Then something in Russian to his translator.

"President Putin says he is curious about this... ballroom project," the translator intoned.

"It's going to be incredible," Trump gushed. "The most beautiful ballroom ever built. I wanted you to see it before anyone else. Well, not see it yet, it's not built yet, but you're the first to audition, which is very special—"

Putin said something brief in Russian.

"President Putin suggests we begin," the translator said.

Michelle gestured to the floor. "Gentlemen, whenever you're ready."

Trump practically bounded forward. Putin moved to the center of the floor with measured steps.

"So, uh, I'll lead," Trump said. "That's traditional. The man leads."

Putin tilted his head slightly. "In Russia, the stronger man leads."

"Right, yes, that's what I meant. I'm very strong. Everyone says so. Strongest president we've ever had."

Putin extended his hand, but positioned himself in the lead position.

"Wait," Trump said. "I thought I was—"

"In ballroom dancing," Putin said in careful English, "the leader must establish dominance first. Perhaps we see who is better suited."

Michelle made a note: Three seconds in and already a power struggle.

Trump hesitated, then took the follower's position, his face reddening. "Just for a moment. To see the technique."

The pianist began a tango - Michelle's choice, deliberate and aggressive.

Putin led with absolute precision, his movements controlled and clinical. He guided Trump through the steps with firm pressure, military in its exactness. Trump stumbled trying to keep up.

"You must trust your partner," Putin said. "Surrender control."

"I'm very good at trust," Trump said, breathless. "The best at trust."

Putin executed a sharp turn, yanking Trump with such force that he nearly lost his balance. Michelle watched Trump's face cycle through confusion, embarrassment, and something that looked almost like... pleasure at being dominated.

"In Russia," Putin continued, leading Trump backward across the floor, "we teach children to dance from young age. Discipline. Control. Precision." He spun Trump out, then pulled him back with a jerk. "These are not suggestions. These are requirements."

"I could do this," Trump said. "If I was leading, I'd be tremendous at this."

"Perhaps we switch," Putin said, releasing him.

They repositioned, Trump now in the lead. The pianist started again.

Trump immediately tried to replicate Putin's forceful style, yanking and pushing. But where Putin had been controlled, Trump was chaotic. He pulled when he should have guided, shoved when he should have led.

"You are trying too hard," Putin observed, allowing himself to be manhandled around the floor. "Leadership is not about force.

Is about making the follower believe they have choice when they do not."

"I'm a tremendous leader," Trump panted. "I've led billions of people. Millions. A lot of people."

"Yes," Putin said, his expression unreadable. "You have led many people exactly where I wanted them to go."

Trump missed the subtext entirely. "See? You understand. We understand each other, Vladimir. We have chemistry."

Michelle's pen moved rapidly across her page.

Putin executed a sudden reversal, somehow regaining the lead position mid-step. Trump found himself being guided backward again without quite understanding how it happened.

"The tango," Putin said, "is like geopolitics. One partner appears to follow, but both are trying to control the dance. The question is: who is better at hiding their control?"

He maneuvered Trump into a dramatic dip. Trump went backward, off-balance, completely at Putin's mercy. For a long moment, Putin held him there, Trump's combover dangling, his face vulnerable.

"Trust," Putin said softly, "is dangerous thing, Donald."

Then he pulled Trump upright with a jerk.

Trump straightened his jacket, breathing hard. "That was... that was really good, Vladimir. Really tremendous. Did you see that, Michelle? That was like professional level."

Putin turned to Michelle, ignoring Trump. "Mrs. Obama. Your husband was adequate dancer. Not great, but adequate. He understood something important."

"What's that?" Michelle asked.

"That in a partnership, sometimes appearing to follow is the greatest show of strength." He looked at Trump. "Your president has not learned this lesson."

"I'm a great follower," Trump protested. "When I need to be. Which isn't often, but I can do it. I just showed you."

Putin said something to his translator in Russian. She spoke: "President Putin says the audition is complete. He will await Mrs. Obama's decision."

"Wait," Trump said. "Don't you want to go again? We were just getting warmed up. We could try a different dance. A waltz maybe. I'm better at waltzes."

Putin was already moving toward the door. He paused, turned back. "Donald. In Russia, we have saying: 'The fish always rots from the head.' You are building very expensive ballroom. Very beautiful, I am sure. But ballroom without true partner?" He shrugged. "Is just expensive room."

After the Russians left, Trump turned to Michelle triumphantly. "He loved it! Did you hear him? He said my ballroom was beautiful!"

"He said it would be beautiful," Michelle corrected. "And he called you a rotting fish head."

"No, no, that was a Russian compliment. A saying about leadership. Vladimir and I, we speak the same language."

Michelle closed her portfolio. "Mr. President, that was perhaps the most disturbing thing I've witnessed in my eight years in this building."

"Disturbing? It was tremendous! We had real chemistry. Did you see how well we moved together?"

"I saw him lead you around like a puppet on strings while you thanked him for it."

"That's called diplomacy, Michelle. Strategic following. Very advanced concept."

Michelle stood, gathering her things. "I need to go home and shower. Possibly in bleach."

"So he's in the running, right? For the first dance?"

Michelle stopped at the door. "Mr. President, if I select Vladimir Putin as your dance partner, it will be because I want the entire world to see exactly what I just witnessed."

"Great!" Trump beamed. "That's great! See, I told you he was perfect!"

After Michelle left, Trump stood alone in the East Room, humming the tango, practicing the steps Putin had led him through. In his mind, he was leading. In his mind, he had won.

He was still practicing when a Secret Service agent gently suggested he had a noon meeting.

"Tell them to wait," Trump said. "I'm working on something important. Vladimir said I needed to work on my trust. My surrender."

The agent exchanged a glance with his partner.

"Sir, it's a meeting with the Joint Chiefs."

"They can wait," Trump said, attempting Putin's dramatic dip on an imaginary partner. "This is about national security too. Ballroom security."

# Chapter 6
# Lindsey Graham's Audition

Michelle Obama had learned to keep a bottle of Advil in her portfolio. By this time, she realized she was going to need it.

Senator Lindsey Graham arrived twenty minutes early, bustling into the East Room with the energy of a golden retriever who'd been promised a car ride. He wore a powder blue tuxedo that looked like it had been ordered from a 1987 prom catalog.

"Mrs. Obama! What an honor, what an absolute honor!" He clasped her hand with both of his, pumping enthusiastically. "You look radiant. Just radiant. Doesn't she look radiant?" He looked around for confirmation, but they were alone except for the pianist.

"Senator Graham," Michelle said, extracting her hand. "Thank you for coming."

"Are you kidding? When the President asks Lindsey Graham to audition for the most important dance in American history—maybe world history—Lindsey Graham shows up! Early! With bells on!" He gestured to his tuxedo. "Metaphorical bells. Though I could get actual bells if the President would prefer bells."

Michelle made a note: *Dear Lord.*

Trump strode in, and Graham's face transformed into something between worship and hunger.

"Mr. President! Sir! You look magnificent! Is that a new tuxedo? The cut is perfection. The fit is perfection. You are perfection, sir!"

"Lindsey!" Trump seemed genuinely pleased. "You wore the blue tuxedo. That's bold. Very bold."

"You once said blue was a strong color, sir. I remembered that. I remember everything you say. I have a whole notebook—"

"Senator," Michelle interrupted. "Shall we begin?"

"Yes! Yes, of course! I'm ready, Mr. President. I've been practicing. I hired a professional instructor. I watched YouTube videos. I studied the great dancers—Astaire, Kelly, that fellow from Strictly Come Dancing. I am PREPARED, sir!"

The pianist began a foxtrot. Graham practically lunged at Trump, seizing his hand.

"I'll follow, naturally!" Graham announced. "I'm an excellent follower. The best follower. Following is my greatest skill!"

Trump took the lead position, and they began to move. Graham's technique was actually competent—he'd clearly practiced—but his commentary was relentless.

"Oh, Mr. President, your posture! So straight! So commanding!"

"Well, I do have good posture—"

"The best posture! Presidential posture! When you stand like that, I can practically hear 'Hail to the Chief' playing!"

They turned, Graham executing the steps perfectly while gazing up at Trump with alarming intensity.

"Your hand placement, sir, is textbook. Textbook! But also better than textbook because you wrote the textbook!"

Michelle closed her eyes briefly.

"And your leading, Mr. President—so decisive! So firm! I know exactly where you want me to go, and I want to go there too! I've always wanted to go where you want me to go!"

"Lindsey, you're doing good—"

"Good? GOOD? Sir, this is transcendent! This is the pinnacle of my life! When I'm old—older—and I'm telling my grandnieces and grandnephews about my accomplishments, I will say: 'Children, I once danced with the greatest president in American history. Possibly the greatest man in American history!'"

Trump attempted a turn. Graham spun with excessive enthusiasm, nearly losing his balance.

"MAGNIFICENT!" Graham gasped. "The centrifugal force! The grace! Sir, you could have been a professional dancer if you hadn't been busy saving America!"

"I did consider it—"

"Of course you did! You could have done anything! But you chose to serve! You chose to lead! And now you're leading me across this dance floor, and it's the greatest honor of my life!"

They continued moving, Graham's praise building like a symphony reaching crescendo.

"Your rhythm, sir! Impeccable! You're like a metronome, if metronomes were tall and handsome and ran for president!"

Michelle's pen was moving so fast the page was smoking.

"The way you guide me backward—so confident! I would follow you backward off a cliff, sir! I have followed you backward off several metaphorical cliffs, and I would do it again!"

"Lindsey, maybe dial it back a little—"

"NEVER! I will never dial back my admiration for you, sir! When they write the history books—and they will write many, many history books about you—there will be a footnote about how Lindsey Graham was honored to be considered as your dance partner!"

Trump attempted a more complex step. Graham anticipated it, moving in perfect sync.

"You see that, Mrs. Obama? Perfect synchronization! That's because I'm attuned to the President's every move! I watch C-SPAN replays of his speeches! I follow his Truth Social posts! I set alerts! I know his rhythms, his patterns, his preferred angles of approach!"

"That's... unsettling," Michelle murmured.

"It's DEDICATION!" Graham corrected, executing a perfect chassé. "When you love someone's leadership as much as I love the President's leadership, you study it! You memorize it! You dream about it!"

"Okay, that's definitely unsettling," Trump said.

Graham continued, undeterred. "Mr. President, if you select me as your dance partner, I promise you—I PROMISE YOU—I will make you look so good that people will forget you ever had any other dance partners! They'll say, 'Trump and Graham, what a pair! Better than Rogers and Astaire! Better than Romeo and Juliet!'"

"Romeo and Juliet weren't dancers—" Michelle started.

"THEY SHOULD HAVE BEEN! With the President leading, anything is possible!"

Trump attempted to end the dance, but Graham held on.

"Just one more turn, sir! Please! I've waited my whole life for this moment!"

"Lindsey, the song is over."

"So what? We make our own music! We always have! You play the Trump card, and I play whatever card helps the Trump card!"

Michelle stood. "Senator Graham, I think we've seen enough."

Graham finally released Trump, but remained in dance position, arms extended toward empty air. "That was... that was everything I dreamed it would be."

Trump adjusted his tie, looking slightly disturbed. "That was... enthusiastic."

"Sir, if you need me to audition again, I'm available. I'm always available. I've cleared my schedule through 2029. Maybe through 2033, depending on term limits, which are really just suggestions—"

"Senator," Michelle said firmly. "Thank you for your time. We'll be in touch."

"Can I stay and watch the other auditions? I could take notes! I could provide commentary! I could hold your clipboard, Mrs. Obama!"

"That won't be necessary."

"I could just sit quietly in the corner! You wouldn't even know I was there! I'm very good at sitting quietly in corners while the President does things!"

Trump moved toward the door. "Lindsey, go back to the Senate."

"Yes, sir! Right away, sir! Should I vote yes or no on that bill?"

"What bill?"

"Any bill, sir! Just tell me which way you're leaning, and I'll enthusiastically lean that way too!"

After Graham finally left—backing out of the room while still facing Trump and bowing—Michelle sat heavily in her chair.

"That man," she said slowly, "should be studied by psychologists."

Trump shrugged. "Lindsey's loyal. Very loyal. Maybe too loyal."

"He called you his life's purpose."

"He says that a lot."

"He said he dreams about your leadership style."

"That's a little weird," Trump admitted. "But the dancing was good, right? He knew all the steps."

"Mr. President, that man would follow you into active volcano while composing sonnets about the majesty of your decision to jump into an active volcano."

Trump considered this. "So he's a strong candidate?"

Michelle opened her portfolio, added several pages of notes. "If I pick Senator Graham, it will be because I want America to witness the complete absence of dignity in modern politics, set to a foxtrot."

"I'll take that as a yes!"

"That was not a yes."

"Sounded like a yes to me. Put him in the maybe pile. The strong maybe pile."

Michelle watched Trump leave, then turned to the pianist. "Play something sad. Something that captures the death of decorum."

The pianist began a funeral march.

"Perfect," Michelle said, pouring herself a glass of water. "How many more auditions to go?"

# Chapter 7

# Elder Ras Nehemiah Johnson's Audition

Michelle Obama had seen the application essay and immediately moved it to the top of her list. Something about the handwritten submission on worn paper, the careful script, the opening line: "Di dance is di heartbeat a di earth, an' if di president want fi learn di rhythm, him mus' first learn fi listen."

Elder Nehemiah Johnson arrived at the White House on a humid afternoon, wearing simple white linen and carrying nothing but a worn leather bag. No entourage, no security, no demands. He moved through the East Room like water finding its level, entirely at ease in a space that made most people nervous.

Trump entered, stopped short. "You're the dancer? I was expecting... I don't know what I was expecting. Do you have credentials? Dance training?"

"Mi have seventy-tree year a trainin', Mr. President," Nehemiah said, his voice like honey over gravel. "Been dancin' since before yuh born. Been listenin' even longer."

Michelle gestured to chairs. "Elder Johnson, thank you for coming all the way from Jamaica. Can I offer you water? Tea?"

"Water bless, Mrs. Obama. Tank yuh."

Trump paced, checking his watch. "So how does this work? You know the steps? The foxtrot, the waltz?"

"Yuh know what a step is, Mr. President?"

"Of course I know what a step is. I'm an excellent dancer."

"No, bredrin. Not dance step. What a step IS." Nehemiah settled into his chair like a tree taking root. "A step is when yuh foot leave one place an' choose fi go anodda place. Dat a act a fait', seen? Everyting between yuh an' di ground—dat a moment a trust."

Trump looked at Michelle. "Is he going to talk like this the whole time?"

"I certainly hope so," Michelle said, making a note.

Nehemiah smiled, patient as stone. "Mr. President, before wi dance, mi need fi ask yuh someting. Why yuh want dis ballroom?"

"Because the White House needs one. For entertaining, for state dinners, for showing America's greatness."

"But why yuh want it?"

Trump paused. "It's going to be beautiful. The most beautiful ballroom ever built."

"An' when it done, when all di marble lay down an' all di gold hang up, what yuh ago do wid it?"

"Dance in it! That's why we're doing these auditions!"

"No, bredrin. What yuh ago DO wid it? What purpose it serve fi yuh spirit?"

Trump's face reddened. "My spirit? What does my spirit have to do with real estate development?"

Nehemiah stood slowly, moved to the center of the room. "Everyting. Come, mek wi try someting."

"We're dancing now?"

"No, bredrin. We walkin'. Jus' walk wid mi." Nehemiah began to move in a slow circle, his feet barely leaving the ground, his whole body swaying like grass in wind. "Feel di floor under yuh foot. Feel how it hold yuh up. Give tanks fi dat."

Trump walked behind him, stiff and impatient. "This isn't dancing."

"Not yet. First yuh mus' learn fi be present wid yuh body deh. Most people, dem body here but dem mind somewhere else, worried 'bout tomorrow or yesterday. How yuh ago dance if yuh no even here?"

"I'm here. I'm completely here."

Nehemiah stopped, turned to face him. "Den tell mi, Mr. President—what color is Mrs. Obama dress?"

Trump glanced at Michelle, genuinely unsure. "Blue? Is it blue?"

"Gray," Michelle said.

"See?" Nehemiah's eyes twinkled. "Yuh been inna dis room twenty minute, an' yuh no see di woman right in front a yuh. How yuh ago see yuh dance partner when di music start?"

Trump's jaw tightened. "Let's just do the actual dancing."

"As yuh wish." Nehemiah nodded to the pianist, who began something slow and rhythmic, almost like a heartbeat. "Now, inna Rasta tradition, di dance no belong fi di dancer. Di dance belong fi JAH, an' wi jus' di vessel wah carry it. So when yuh dance wid mi, yuh no tryin' fi control di movement—yuh tryin' fi surrender to it."

"I don't surrender," Trump said flatly.

"Mi know. Dat a yuh problem, seen?"

They moved into dance position. Trump tried to lead immediately, pulling and directing.

"Yuh fightin' di rhythm," Nehemiah said softly. "Why yuh always a fight?"

"I'm not fighting, I'm leading."

"No, bredrin. Leadin' is like dis—" Nehemiah somehow shifted the dynamic without apparent effort, guiding Trump through the steps with such subtle pressure that Trump barely noticed he was being led. "Yuh feel dat? Mi no pushin' yuh, mi no pullin' yuh. Mi jus' suggestin', an' yuh body agree 'cause it feel natural."

Trump stumbled, frustrated. "This isn't how I learned."

"How yuh learn?"

"By being strong. By being decisive."

"Strong like oak tree or strong like bamboo?"

"What's the difference?"

"Oak tree stan' firm, no bend. Hurricane come, oak tree break. Bamboo, him bend wid di wind, him flow wid di storm. Hurricane pass, bamboo still standin'. Which one yuh tink is truly strong?"

"The oak," Trump said immediately. "Standing firm shows strength."

Nehemiah smiled sadly. "Den yuh have hurricane comin', Mr. President, an' yuh no even know it yet."

They continued dancing, or rather, Nehemiah continued dancing while Trump struggled against every natural movement. Michelle watched, fascinated, as the elder maintained perfect grace while Trump grew increasingly agitated.

"Why yuh breathin' so hard?" Nehemiah asked. "We barely a move."

"I'm not used to... this is different from regular dancing."

"All dancin' is di same, bredrin. Is all 'bout listenin'. Di music tell yuh someting, yuh partner tell yuh someting, yuh own body tell yuh someting. But yuh cyan hear none a dem 'cause yuh too busy tellin' yuhself how great yuh is."

Trump stopped moving. "Are you insulting me?"

"No, bredrin. Mi observin' yuh. Big difference. Yuh have good posture, yuh have confidence, yuh have ambition. But yuh no have peace. An' widout peace, di dance jus' a exercise. Pretty maybe, but empty."

Michelle's pen moved across the page steadily.

"Tell mi someting," Nehemiah said, releasing Trump and stepping back. "When yuh build dis big ballroom, when all di people come fi see it, when di lights shine an' di music play—what yuh ago feel inna dat moment?"

Trump straightened his jacket. "Pride. Accomplishment. Success."

"An' after di moment pass? When di guest dem gone home, when di music stop, when yuh alone in yuh big empty ballroom—what yuh ago feel den?"

Silence. Long enough that even Trump seemed to notice it.

"Mi tell yuh what," Nehemiah said gently. "Yuh ago feel hungry. Not fi food, not fi drink. Hungry fi someting yuh cyan name, someting yuh spend yuh whole life tryin' fi fill up wid building dem an' money an' people tellin' yuh how great yuh is. But it no work, 'cause what yuh truly hungry fi yuh cyan buy, cyan build, an' cyan get from no person. It only come when yuh stop chasin' an' start listenin'."

Trump's face had gone through several colors. "I think we're done here."

"As yuh wish, Mr. President." Nehemiah collected his bag. "But before mi go, mi leave yuh wid one ting. When yuh inna yuh ballroom, standin' wid whoever yuh choose fi dance wid, remember dis: Di greatest dancer is not di one who move di best. Is di one who mek everybody else feel di music. Seen?"

After he left, Trump turned to Michelle. "That was completely unprofessional. He barely danced. He just talked in riddles."

Michelle closed her portfolio slowly. "He danced the entire time. You just weren't paying attention."

"Well, he's obviously not qualified."

"For what? To dance with you, or to teach you something you desperately need to learn?"

"I don't need lessons from some old—"

"Careful," Michelle said sharply. "That 'old man' has more wisdom in his smallest finger than exists in your entire administration."

"So he's out?"

Michelle stood, gathering her things. "I'll add him to the list."

"The no list?"

"The list of people who actually understand what a dance partnership means."

Trump snorted. "Dancing isn't that deep."

"That," Michelle said, heading for the door, "is exactly why you need more auditions."

Later that evening, Trump called his marble supplier to complain about a delivery delay. Then he posted three times on Truth Social about how the fake news media was ignoring the ballroom project. Then he watched a clip of himself on Fox News and rewound the part where they called him "a visionary" twice.

He never thought about Elder Nehemiah again.

# Chapter 8
# Melania's Audition

The temperature in the East Room had dropped ten degrees before Melania even arrived. Michelle Obama felt it, some atmospheric shift that made her reach for her cardigan. The pianist flexed his fingers nervously.

When Melania entered, she moved like a woman walking through an airport—efficient, disinterested, already planning her exit. She wore a severe black dress that cost more than most cars and expressed less emotion than most furniture.

"Mrs. Trump," Michelle said, standing. "Thank you for—"

"Let us begin," Melania said in her Slovenian-accented English. "I have appointment after."

Trump bounded in, overly enthusiastic. "Melania! You look beautiful! Doesn't she look beautiful, Michelle?"

Melania's expression didn't change. She might have been carved from ice.

"Shall we dance?" Trump reached for her hand.

She allowed him to take it the way one might allow a stranger to check your pulse—necessary, clinical, devoid of intimacy.

The pianist began a waltz. They moved into position with the chemistry of two people waiting for an elevator.

"You've been practicing," Trump said. "I can tell."

Silence.

"The ballroom is going to be spectacular. You'll love it."

More silence.

"Ninety thousand square feet. Gold fixtures. The best marble—"

"I have seen the plans," Melania said flatly. "You showed them to me four times."

They danced with technical precision. Melania's training as a model meant she knew how to move, how to position her body, how to look graceful while feeling nothing. Trump led competently, and that was somehow the saddest thing Michelle had ever witnessed—two people who could dance together perfectly but clearly wished they were dancing with anyone else.

"Remember our wedding?" Trump tried. "We danced to that song, what was it—"

"I do not remember."

"Come on, sure you do. It was that Frank Sinatra song—"

"I have danced to many songs at many events. They blur together."

Michelle made a note: *This is a marriage or a business arrangement?*

Trump's voice took on a pleading quality. "The first dance in the
new ballroom could be special. Like renewing our vows, but with
better music and more cameras—"

"I do not need vows renewed," Melania said, her tone suggesting
she found the original vows more than sufficient, possibly excessive.

They continued in painful silence, executing turns and steps
with the passion of two people filling out tax forms. Melania's face
remained perfectly neutral, her thoughts clearly elsewhere—perhaps mentally redecorating, perhaps planning lunch, perhaps calculating the exact number of minutes until this ordeal ended.

"You could smile," Trump suggested.

"I could," Melania agreed, not smiling.

Trump tried a dip. Melania allowed herself to be dipped with
all the enthusiasm of a mannequin being repositioned in a store
window.

"See? We still have it!" Trump said desperately.

"Have what?"

"Chemistry! That spark!"

Melania's eyebrow raised approximately one millimeter—the
equivalent, for her, of hysterical laughter. "Yes. Much spark."

The music ended. Melania stepped back immediately, putting
exactly the correct amount of social distance between them.

"So," Trump said to Michelle, "that was great, right? We looked
great?"

Before Michelle could respond, the East Room doors opened.

"Oh my GOD, am I early?" Stormy Daniels stood in the doorway, wearing a dress that was considerably less expensive than

Melania's but considerably more... present. "I thought my audition was at three?"

The room temperature somehow dropped another ten degrees while simultaneously catching fire.

Trump's face cycled through several colors not found in nature. "You're—what are you—Michelle, what is she doing here?"

Michelle consulted her schedule with studied calm. "Ms. Daniels submitted an audition application. A very thorough application, actually. Very... detailed."

"I can come back," Stormy said, not moving an inch, clearly enjoying herself. "I wouldn't want to interrupt... whatever this is." She looked at Melania. "Love the dress. Very funeral chic."

Melania's expression didn't change, but something flickered in her eyes—not anger, not hurt, just a kind of weary recognition. She'd known about Stormy. She'd known about all of them. This was merely confirmation of facts already in evidence.

"I vas finished," Melania said, already moving toward the door. She paused next to Stormy. "Good luck. You vill need it."

"Wait!" Trump called. "Melania, don't you want to stay? We should talk about—"

"Ve have nothing to discuss. You have audition." She glanced back at Michelle. "Mrs. Obama, tank you for your time. I trust you vill make... appropriate choice." The way she said "appropriate" suggested she found the entire concept laughable.

Then she was gone, leaving behind the faint scent of expensive perfume and crushing indifference.

Stormy walked into the room, heels clicking on the marble. "Well, that wasn't awkward at all."

Trump's face was red. "You can't be here. This is inappropriate. Michelle, tell her this is inappropriate."

"Actually," Michelle said, flipping through her notes, "Ms. Daniels's application was quite compelling. She has professional dance experience—"

"I can do a lot of things professionally," Stormy interjected.

"—and her essay on why she wanted to be your dance partner was... let's say memorable."

Trump looked like he wanted the floor to swallow him. "What did she write?"

"Would you like me to read it aloud?" Michelle asked, a slight smile playing at her lips.

"NO!"

"I said," Stormy announced, settling into a chair and crossing her legs, "that I already knew what it was like to dance with you, metaphorically speaking, and I figured actual dancing couldn't be any more disappointing."

The pianist made a sound that might have been a cough or a laugh.

"You can't talk to the President like that," Trump sputtered.

"Pretty sure I just did, Mushroom—"

"OKAY!" Michelle stood abruptly. "Ms. Daniels, I think we'll need to reschedule your audition for another time."

"But I'm here now! I wore my best dress and everything." Stormy stood, walked toward Trump, who backed up like she was radioactive. "Come on, Mr. President. One little dance. For old times' sake."

"There were no old times!"

"That's not what you said in—"

"Ms. Daniels," Michelle said firmly, "I believe there's a scheduling conflict. Perhaps next week?"

Stormy shrugged, clearly having gotten what she came for—Trump's discomfort. "Sure. Though between you and me," she said to Michelle, loud enough for Trump to hear, "I don't think he's got the stamina for a full ballroom dance. Thirty seconds, maybe. Forty-five if he's really trying to impress someone."

After she left, Trump stood alone in the East Room, his tuxedo somehow looking more rumpled than before despite no one having touched it.

"That was a setup," he said to Michelle.

"Was it?" Michelle gathered her things. "Or was it just the inevitable consequence of your choices catching up with you at the worst possible moment?"

"You scheduled them at the same time on purpose!"

"Actually, Ms. Daniels was scheduled for 3:00 PM. She arrived at 2:45. I can't control when people show up early." Michelle's face was innocent. "Though I admit, I didn't try very hard to prevent the overlap."

Trump slumped into a chair. "Melania hates me."

"I don't think she hates you. Hate requires caring."

"That's worse."

"Yes," Michelle agreed. "It really is."

She headed for the door, then paused. "For what it's worth, you and Melania actually danced quite well together. Technically perfect. Completely soulless, but technically perfect."

"So she's still in the running?"

Michelle considered this. "Mr. President, if I choose Melania as your dance partner, it will be because I want the world to see exactly what your marriage looks like—impeccably choreographed, flawlessly executed, and completely devoid of joy."

"Is that a yes?"

"It's an observation. I have more auditions to watch before I decide anything."

After Michelle left, Trump was already on his phone.

*Stormy Daniels showed up UNINVITED to the White House today. Very desperate! Still trying to be relevant. SAD! Security has been notified. The auditions are going VERY WELL despite interference from losers and haters!*

He texted Melania: "You were great today."

No response.

He didn't notice. He was already calling his ballroom contractor about upgrading the chandeliers.

# Chapter 9
# Mike Pence's Audition

Michelle Obama noticed two things immediately: the reinforced collar around Mike Pence's neck, and the woman sitting in a chair he'd brought with him.

"Mr. Vice President," Michelle said. "Thank you for coming. And this is...?"

"Mother," Pence said, gesturing to Karen Pence, who sat rigidly in a straight-backed chair she'd apparently carried into the East

Room herself. She wore a floral dress and an expression of profound disapproval. "She's here to supervise."

"Supervise what?"

"The dancing. Mother has concerns."

Karen Pence nodded once, lips pressed into a thin line.

Trump entered, stopped when he saw the setup. "Mike. What's with the neck thing? And why is Karen here?"

"The collar is a precaution, sir. In case anyone tries to hang me again."

"That was years ago—"

"And Mother is here because I'll be dancing with another man." Pence's smile was fixed, unsettling. "She has rules."

Karen Pence produced a laminated card from her purse and held it up. Michelle squinted to read it: **MOTHER'S GUIDELINES FOR ACCEPTABLE MALE-TO-MALE PHYSICAL CONTACT.**

"There are rules?" Trump asked.

"Seventeen," Karen said. It was the first word she'd spoken. It might be the last.

"Perhaps we should begin," Michelle suggested.

Pence approached Trump slowly, like a man walking toward a sleeping lion. He stopped approximately three feet away.

"Closer," Michelle said.

Pence looked at Mother. She consulted her laminated card, then shook her head.

"This is as close as the guidelines permit," Pence explained. "Rule four: maintain a distance of no less than thirty-six inches during upright dancing."

"You can't waltz from three feet apart," Trump said.

"Mother and I discussed this. We've developed a modification." Pence produced two wooden dowels, each about eighteen inches long. "We hold these between us. That way we maintain proper distance while still technically dancing together."

"I'm not holding sticks."

"They're dowels, sir. Blessed by our pastor."

Michelle made a note: *I should have charged admission.*

Trump knocked the dowels aside. "We're dancing like normal people. Karen, look away or something."

"Mother doesn't look away," Pence said. "Mother watches. It's rule one."

Karen Pence's gaze intensified.

The pianist began a waltz. Trump grabbed Pence's hand. Pence immediately closed his eyes.

"What are you doing?" Trump demanded.

"If I can't see it, it's less sinful. Mother and I agreed on this compromise."

"You can't dance with your eyes closed!"

"I danced with my eyes closed at our wedding," Pence said serenely. "Mother guided me verbally."

"Left," Karen called out. "Left. Right. Back. You're too close, Michael."

"I'm four inches away!"

"That's three inches too close. Rule seven."

Trump tried to lead Pence into a turn. Pence resisted, his body rigid as a diving board.

"You have to move with me," Trump said.

"I am moving, sir. I'm moving within the guidelines."

"You're shuffling like a robot!"

"Robots don't have souls to imperil, Mr. President. I do."

They continued their strange approximation of dancing—Trump pulling, Pence resisting, Karen calling out corrections from her chair like a GPS navigation system with a theology degree.

"Forward. Forward. Too much hip movement, Michael."

"Sorry, Mother."

"Is that your hand on his shoulder blade? That's very close to his lower back."

"It's the standard waltz position—" Trump started.

"There's nothing standard about two men dancing," Karen said flatly. "Rule twelve."

Michelle watched, transfixed. The pianist had given up trying to match their tempo and was simply playing random waltz music while they lurched around the floor.

"Michael, you're making a face," Karen called.

"What face?" Pence asked, eyes still closed.

"The face you made when the cat died. Mournful. Less mournful, please. People will think you're enjoying this."

"I'm not enjoying this, Mother."

"I know, dear. But your face doesn't know."

Trump stopped moving. "This is insane. Mike, open your eyes. Karen, stop talking. We're going to dance like adults."

Pence's eyes snapped open. He looked at Mother. She gave a nearly imperceptible nod.

"Mother has granted a five-minute exception to rules four, seven, and twelve," Pence announced. "But rule sixteen remains in effect."

"What's rule sixteen?"

"No dipping. Under any circumstances. Dipping leads to closeness. Closeness leads to familiarity. Familiarity leads to..." He trailed off, glancing at Karen.

"Sin," Karen finished. "Dipping leads to sin."

"I wasn't going to dip you!" Trump exclaimed.

"You dipped some of the others. Mother saw the footage."

"That was different!"

"Sin doesn't differentiate, sir."

They resumed dancing, marginally more functional now that Pence's eyes were open. But Pence held himself like a man being escorted to the gallows—which, Michelle reflected, was perhaps understandable given his history with Trump.

"You're still very stiff," Trump complained.

"Looseness is suspect, sir. Rule three."

"How many rules ARE there?"

"Seventeen for dancing. Forty-three for general life. Two hundred and six for travel."

Karen nodded confirmation.

Trump attempted to guide Pence into a simple spin. Pence executed it mechanically, arms pinned to his sides, expression unchanged.

"That wasn't a spin," Trump said. "That was a rotation."

"Spins are flamboyant, sir. Mother prefers rotations."

"Mother prefers rotations," Karen echoed.

Michelle realized she had stopped taking notes and was simply staring.

"Michael, your tie is touching his tie," Karen announced.

Pence leaped backward as if burned. "I'm sorry, Mother. It won't happen again."

"Ties touching is rule nine," Pence explained to Trump. "It's considered a gateway."

"A gateway to WHAT?"

"We don't discuss it."

The music ended. Pence immediately retreated to stand beside Karen's chair, hands clasped, smile restored.

"How did I do, Mother?"

Karen consulted a small notebook she'd been writing in. "Three rule violations. The tie incident. Excessive eye contact at minute two. And your left hand migrated above the equator."

"Above the what?" Trump asked.

"Mother has divided the human body into hemispheres," Pence explained. "For safety."

"The equator is the belt line," Karen added. "Nothing above the equator except during medical emergencies."

Trump looked at Michelle desperately.

Michelle cleared her throat. "Well, I think we've seen enough—"

"Wait," Pence said. "I should mention that if selected, Mother would need to attend the grand opening. With her chair. And she'll need a clear sightline to the dance floor."

"She's not coming to my ballroom with a chair."

"Then I'm afraid I'll have to withdraw, sir." Pence didn't seem upset by this. "Mother's supervision is non-negotiable. I made a vow."

"When?"

"1985. Before we could date. I signed a covenant."

"You signed a contract to have your wife watch you forever?"

"It's laminated," Karen said, patting her purse.

After the Pences left—Karen carrying her chair, Mike carrying her backup laminated cards—Trump stood in the center of the East Room looking genuinely shaken.

"That was the strangest thing I've ever seen," he said. "And I've seen a lot of strange things. Putin strange. Kim Jong Un strange. But that..." He shook his head. "Mother is terrifying."

"Mother is committed," Michelle corrected.

"She had a NOTEBOOK. She was grading him!"

"Some marriages are partnerships, Mr. President. Others are supervision arrangements."

Trump was already on his phone, posting to Truth Social:

*Just had a VERY STRANGE audition with Mike Pence and his wife who he calls "Mother" (weird!). She brought her own chair and had a list of RULES about dancing. Too complicated! Some people aren't meant for ballrooms. I like people who weren't almost hanged!*

He looked up. "That last line is good, right? Punchy."

"It references you trying to have him killed, Mr. President."

"It references him FAILING. Big difference."

He pocketed his phone and headed for the door. "Who's next? Please tell me it's someone normal."

Michelle flipped through her notes. "Do we have any normal ones?"

# Chapter 10

# Madison's Audition (@MadisonVibes)

Michelle Obama looked at the application essay one more time: *OMG so like, I totally want to dance with the president because like, my grandma says he's super famous? And also it would be like, SO good for my socials? I have like 47K followers on TikTok and my engagement rate is literally insane rn. Also I can dance? Like, I've*

*been dancing since I was like, five? So yeah that's why I should be picked, periodt.*

Michelle had almost rejected it. Then she'd thought: *Why not? Let's see what happens.*

Madison arrived in a crop top, high-waisted jeans, and white sneakers that cost more than most people's monthly rent. She had her phone out before she fully entered the East Room, filming herself.

"OMG you guys, I'm literally at the White House right now? Like, the actual White House? This is so aesthetic." She panned the camera around the room. "The vibes in here are like, giving historical, you know?"

Michelle stood. "Madison?"

"Oh hi! Are you like, the coordinator person?" Madison put her phone in her back pocket—sort of. It was still recording. "This place is literally so bougie. Like, the ceilings? Insane."

"I'm Michelle Obama."

Madison's eyes went wide. "Shut UP. Like, THE Michelle Obama? From like, the memes?"

"From... being First Lady, yes."

"OMG I love you! You're like, iconic? My mom talks about you literally all the time. She says you had the best arms? Which like, slay."

Trump entered, stopped when he saw Madison. "Who's this?"

"I'm Madison? I'm here for the audition thing?" She pulled out her phone again, aimed it at Trump. "Wait, can I get a video? My followers are gonna literally die."

"Put the phone away," Trump said. "No phones during auditions."

"But like, nobody's gonna believe I met you? The guy from The Apprentice?"

Trump's face brightened. "You watched The Apprentice?"

"No, but my mom did? She said you were like, super mean to people? Which is lowkey iconic."

"I was tough. Tough but fair."

"Yeah, she said you were like, 'You're fired!' all the time?" Madison did an impression that sounded nothing like Trump. "That's so random."

Trump looked at Michelle. "What is she saying?"

"She's saying your catchphrase was memorable."

"Oh. Good." He turned back to Madison. "So you want to dance with the President?"

"I mean, yeah? Like, for my content? Also my grandma says you're like, running the country or whatever, which is cool I guess."

"Running the country is very cool. The most important job in the world."

"That's lit. Okay so like, what kind of dance are we doing? Please don't say ballroom because like, that's giving retirement home, no offense."

"It's a ballroom audition. For my ballroom."

"Oh." Madison looked disappointed. "So like, not TikTok dances?"

"What's a TikTok dance?"

Madison stared at him. "Are you serious right now?"

"What?"

"TikTok? The app? With like, the dances?" She started doing something with her arms that looked vaguely like sign language having a seizure. "Like this? The renegade?"

Trump looked at Michelle helplessly.

"It's a social media platform," Michelle explained. "Popular with young people."

"I don't do social media. I do Truth Social."

"What's Truth Social?" Madison asked.

The pianist began a waltz before anyone could answer. Madison approached Trump, still half-filming with her phone.

"Phone AWAY," Trump said.

"Fine, but like, this is literally a wasted opportunity for both of us? You could go so viral."

"I don't want to go viral. I want to dance."

"Okay but like, have you considered that going viral would be good for your brand?"

"My brand is fine!"

They moved into dance position. Madison looked down at their joined hands.

"Um, so like, this is giving very formal? Are we like, ballroom dancing for real?"

"Yes!"

"Okay but like, I'm gonna be honest? I only know TikTok dances and like, the stuff from dance team in high school? We did not cover whatever this is."

"It's a waltz!"

"A what now?"

"WALTZ. One-two-three, one-two-three."

"Oh like, counting? Okay yeah I can count. One, two, three, four—"

"THREE. Just to three."

"But like, why though?"

Trump looked at Michelle again. "Is she speaking English?"

"Technically," Michelle said, making notes.

They began to move, though "move" was generous. Madison kept trying to add little flourishes—hand movements, hip sways, something she called "hitting the woah"—that had nothing to do with waltzing.

"What are you doing with your arms?" Trump demanded.

"I'm like, adding flavor? You're lowkey really stiff."

"I'm dancing properly!"

"You're dancing like a robot. Like, giving very much AI-generated content."

"What does that even mean?"

"It means you're like, not organic? Your movements are serving nothing."

Trump stopped. "Michelle, what is she saying?"

Michelle consulted her mental database of conversations with Sasha and Malia. "She's saying your dancing lacks authenticity and emotional resonance."

"I'M VERY AUTHENTIC!"

"Okay but like, are you though?" Madison tilted her head. "Because like, the energy you're giving right now is very defensive? Which is like, not the vibe."

"What vibe should I be giving?"

"I don't know, like, confident? Secure? Main character energy?"

"I AM the main character! I'm the President!"

"Yeah but like, you could be the president and still have no rizz? They're not mutually exclusive."

Trump turned to Michelle, desperate. "What's rizz?"

"Charisma," Michelle translated. "She's saying you lack charisma."

"I have tremendous charisma! Everyone says so!"

"Do they though?" Madison asked. "Like, be honest. Are people actually saying that or are you just like, manifesting it?"

They continued their painful approximation of dancing. Madison kept checking her phone, which she'd somehow gotten back out.

"What are you doing?" Trump asked.

"Posting? Like, live? My followers are literally freaking out."

"You're posting DURING the audition?"

"Well yeah, like, otherwise what's the point? If you don't document it, did it even happen?"

"I'm documenting it! Michelle is documenting it! We have a pianist documenting it!"

"Yeah but like, they're not on TikTok? So it's basically the same as not documenting it."

Trump tried to lead her into a turn. Madison spun, but then kept spinning, and then did a little jump, and then struck a pose.

"What was THAT?" Trump asked.

"A transition? For the content? You're supposed to hold the pose so I can like, capture it?"

"We're DANCING, not taking PICTURES!"

"But like, why not both?"

"Because you can't dance while taking pictures!"

"I literally can though? Watch." Madison held her phone at arm's length, started filming, and attempted to waltz while maintaining the camera angle. "See? Like, this is gonna get so many views."

Trump snatched the phone. "NO MORE PHONE!"

"Um, like, that's literally my property? You can't just take someone's phone? That's giving authoritarian."

"I'm not authoritarian, I'm the PRESIDENT!"

"Those aren't opposites?" Madison looked at Michelle. "Are those opposites?"

Michelle was writing so fast her hand was cramping.

Trump handed back the phone. "Fine. Keep the phone. But can you please just dance normally for thirty seconds? Thirty seconds of regular dancing?"

"Okay but like, define normal? Because like, normal is different for everyone? Like, what's normal for you might be giving totally unhinged for me, you know?"

"Normal is—" Trump gestured vaguely. "Moving to the music. Together. Without talking about views and content and—what was the other thing?"

"Rizz?"

"That. Without talking about that."

"Okay." Madison put her phone away. "I can do thirty seconds."

They danced. For approximately ten seconds, it almost looked like actual dancing. Madison followed the steps competently enough, Trump led without shouting.

Then Madison's phone buzzed.

"Oh my god, that's literally Kaylee. She's been commenting on my stories—can I just—"

"NO!"

"But like, she never comments? This is huge?"

"THE AUDITION IS HUGE!"

"I mean, for you maybe."

Trump stopped dancing entirely. "Get out."

"What?"

"Out. Leave. This audition is over."

"Wait, like, for real? You're literally kicking me out?"

"Yes!"

"That's so random." Madison pulled out her phone, started filming again. "You guys, I literally just got kicked out of the White House? By the president? This is insane." She headed for the door, narrating to her phone. "So like, I came here to audition for this dance thing? And he was giving very much boomer energy? Like, didn't even know what TikTok was? Which is honestly concerning for someone who's supposed to be running the country?"

"I KNOW WHAT TIKTOK IS!" Trump shouted after her.

"Okay but like, do you though?" Madison's voice echoed from the hallway. "Because you literally called it 'the TikToks' earlier? Which is so—"

The door closed.

Trump stood in the center of the East Room, breathing hard, looking more rattled than he had after any previous audition.

"What," he said slowly, "was that?"

"That was Generation Z," Michelle said.

"They're all like that?"

"A significant percentage, yes."

"How do they communicate? How do they function?"

"They manage. Somehow."

Trump pulled out his phone, started typing, then stopped. "What's 'rizz'?"

"You don't want to know."

"And 'giving'? She kept saying things were 'giving' other things. What does that mean?"

"It's complicated."

"And why does everything sound like a question? Every sentence went up at the end?"

"That's called upspeak. It's been around since the '80s, but they've perfected it."

Trump sat down heavily. "I'm old."

"Yes."

"When did that happen?"

"Gradually, then suddenly. Like bankruptcy."

Trump stared at his phone. Started to post something about Madison, then stopped. "What if I post something and she responds and I don't understand it and everyone makes fun of me?"

"That's a very real possibility."

"What if all the young people are like her?"

"Not all. But many."

"How do we reach them?"

"We don't, Mr. President. They exist in a completely different reality. We're just visiting."

Trump stood, straightened his tie. "Put her in the no pile."

"She was already in the no pile before she arrived."

"Good." He headed for the door, then turned back. "What's 'periodt'?"

"It means 'end of discussion.' But with emphasis."

"That's stupid."

"Welcome to being old, Mr. President. Periodt."

After he left, Michelle sat alone, reviewing her notes. Her phone buzzed. A text from Malia: *OMG Mom, did you meet Madison? She's posting about you. Says you're "giving iconic energy." That's good.*

Michelle smiled and texted back: *I'm relevant to the youths?*

Malia: *Let's not go that far. But you're not giving cringe, which is something.*

Michelle added a final note: *Madison—eliminated because neither Trump nor I understand what she's saying. Also, she has better social media skills than the entire White House communications team. Should be concerning but honestly just makes me tired.*

She closed her portfolio. Plenty more auditions to go.

She really needed a vacation.

# Chapter 11

# Justin Trudeau's Audition

Michelle Obama noticed that Melania Trump had shown up unannounced for the first time since her own audition. She sat in a chair against the wall, wearing sunglasses indoors, legs crossed, scrolling through her phone with what might have been actual interest instead of her usual performative boredom.

"Mrs. Trump," Michelle said carefully. "I didn't know you were attending today's audition."

"I heard who vas auditioning." Melania didn't look up from her phone. "Thought I vould vatch."

"You didn't watch any of the other auditions."

"The others vere not interesting."

Michelle made a note: *Oh no.*

Trump entered, stopped when he saw Melania. "What are you doing here?"

"Vatching."

"You didn't watch the others."

"They vere boring." She finally looked up, pulled down her sunglasses slightly. "This von vill not be boring."

Trump's jaw tightened. "It's just Trudeau. Nothing special. Just another failed leader who's jealous of American success."

"If you say so." Melania went back to her phone, the smallest smile playing at her lips.

The doors opened. Justin Trudeau walked in looking like he'd stepped out of a cologne advertisement. Perfectly tailored suit, hair that somehow looked casually perfect, the kind of smile that showed up in dentistry textbooks. He moved with the easy confidence of someone who'd never doubted his place in the world.

"Mrs. Obama," he said warmly, taking her hand. "What an honor. Your work on childhood nutrition was groundbreaking."

"Mr. Prime Minister, thank you for coming."

"Justin, please. And I guess I come here as the former Prime Minister." He turned to Trump. "Donald."

"It's Mr. President," Trump said stiffly.

"Of course. Mr. President." Trudeau's smile didn't flicker. He glanced at Melania. "Mrs. Trump, lovely to see you again."

Melania lowered her sunglasses completely. "Prime Minister. You look vell."

"As do you. That's a beautiful dress."

"Thank you. I thought I vould vear something special today."

Trump's face was reddening. "Can we start? I'm very busy. Running a country. The most important country."

"Absolutely." Trudeau moved to the center of the floor with the fluid grace of someone who'd probably taken actual dance lessons. "Shall we?"

Trump stomped over. They faced each other—Trudeau relaxed and smiling, Trump rigid with barely controlled hostility.

The pianist began a foxtrot. Trudeau extended his hand.

"I'll lead," Trump said immediately.

"Of course. I'm a guest in your country." Trudeau smoothly assumed the follower's position.

They began to dance. Within three steps, the difference was obvious. Trudeau moved like he'd been born dancing—smooth, effortless, anticipating Trump's movements before Trump even made them. He made following look easy, which somehow made Trump's leading look harder.

"You've done this before," Trump said accusingly.

"I took some lessons growing up. Ballet, jazz, ballroom. My mother thought it was important."

"Ballet," Trump sneered. "Very manly."

"I found it quite physically demanding, actually. Have you ever tried ballet?"

"I don't need ballet. I'm naturally athletic. The best athlete in any room."

Trudeau glanced at Michelle, then at Melania, as if to say *Is he serious?* He was too polite to say it aloud.

They continued dancing. Trudeau's technique was flawless. Trump kept trying to lead more forcefully, but Trudeau simply flowed with it, making even Trump's roughness look almost intentional.

"You know," Trump said, "people say you're not a real leader. That you're just a pretty face. All style, no substance."

"People say many things." Trudeau executed a perfect turn. "I try not to let it affect my dancing."

"I bet you practice this. I bet you practice looking good all the time."

"I do try to stay in shape. Boxing, mostly. Some yoga. Running."

"I don't need exercise. I have good genes. The best genes. My doctor says I'm the healthiest president ever."

"That's wonderful." Trudeau's tone suggested he found this claim adorable rather than credible.

From her chair, Melania made a small sound that might have been a laugh.

Trump's grip tightened. "What's funny?"

"Nothing," Melania said. "Just remembering something."

"What?"

"Private joke." She smiled at Trudeau. "You are dancing very vell, Prime Minister."

"Thank you, Mrs. Trump. You're very kind."

"Some people just have natural grace," Melania said, still looking at Trudeau. "It cannot be taught."

Trump nearly stumbled. "I have natural grace!"

"Of course you do, dear." Melania went back to her phone.

Michelle was writing furiously: *This is either going to end in an international incident or the most viewed audition footage in history.*

Trump tried a more complex step, something he'd clearly seen in a movie. Trudeau adjusted seamlessly, making it work despite Trump's clumsy execution.

"You're making me look bad on purpose," Trump hissed.

"I'm following your lead, Mr. President. If anything, I'm making you look better than you are."

"What's that supposed to mean?"

"It means I'm a very good follower." Trudeau's smile was pleasant, his tone light, but there was something sharp underneath. "Some might say I'm making you look competent."

"I AM competent!"

"Then there's nothing to worry about."

They spun—Trudeau made it look like a scene from a ballroom competition, Trump made it look like he was trying to escape a wrestling hold.

"Melania," Trump called out, "are you watching this?"

"Mm-hmm." She wasn't looking up from her phone.

"See how well I'm dancing?"

"I see many things." She glanced up briefly. "Prime Minister, your posture is excellent."

"Years of practice, I'm afraid."

"It shows." Was she... was she flirting? Michelle couldn't quite tell, but Trump certainly thought so.

"Maybe we should switch," Trump said suddenly. "I'll follow, you lead. See how YOU do."

"If you'd like." They swapped positions.

The difference was immediate and devastating. Trudeau led with such subtle confidence that even Trump's flailing looked almost intentional. Every movement was clear, gentle, perfectly timed. He was making Trump look better than Trump had ever looked while dancing.

Which somehow made Trump even angrier.

"You're showing off," Trump muttered.

"I'm dancing, Mr. President."

"You're making a point."

"The only point I'm making is that dancing is about partnership. Trust. Mutual respect." He guided Trump through a turn that actually worked. "When you trust your partner, amazing things can happen."

"I don't trust anybody."

"I know. That's why you're having trouble finding a dance partner."

From across the room, Melania's voice: "He speaks the truth."

"Melania!" Trump snapped.

"Vhat? He does." She'd put her phone down and was actually watching now. "Continue, please. This is much better than Netflix."

Michelle added to her notes: *Melania Trump is enjoying her husband's humiliation more than anything I've ever seen.*

The music ended. Trudeau stepped back, perfect smile in place. "Thank you, Mr. President. That was enlightening."

"Enlightening how?"

"It's always educational to dance with someone so... confident in their abilities regardless of actual skill level."

Trump's face went through several colors. "Get out."

"I'm sorry?"

"Out. This audition is over. You're too... you're just not right for this."

"May I ask why?"

"You're too tall. Too good-looking. Too... Canadian. It wouldn't work."

"Too Canadian." Trudeau's smile widened. "I've been called many things, but that's a new one."

He turned to Melania. "Mrs. Trump, it was lovely to see you."

"The pleasure vas mine, Prime Minister. Perhaps ve vill see each other again soon."

"Perhaps we will."

He shook Michelle's hand, nodded to Trump, and left with the same easy grace he'd arrived with.

After the door closed, the room was silent except for Melania's heels clicking as she stood up.

"That vas very entertaining," she said.

"He was showing off," Trump muttered.

"He vas showing competence. Different thing." Melania walked toward the door. "Maybe you should take lessons, Donald. From someone like him."

"I don't need lessons from HIM."

"From anyone, then. You are not as good at dancing as you think you are. Or at many other things." She paused at the door. "But you already know this, I think."

After she left, Trump turned to Michelle. "That was a setup."

"How was it a setup?"

"You invited him knowing Melania would come watch. You're trying to embarrass me."

"Mr. President, I didn't tell Melania who was auditioning today. She figured it out on her own."

"Well, he's out. Completely out. Put him in the never pile."

"There is no 'never pile.'"

"Make one. For him." Trump was already on his phone. "And I'm canceling the Canada thing."

"What Canada thing?"

"All of it. The trade. The border. Everything. They want to be the 51st state? Now they can't. They're banned. Trudeau's banned."

He stormed out, posting to Truth Social as he walked:

*Just had very strange audition with Justin Trudeau (CANADA). Showed up in tight pants trying to show off. Very weird! Melania was there but left early because she was SO BORED. Trudeau is a terrible dancer and a worse leader. His country is falling apart but he has time for ballroom dancing? Sad! Canada is no longer invited to be the 51st state!*

Michelle sat alone, reviewing her notes. She added one final line: *Trudeau—eliminated because he made Trump look bad simply by existing. Also because Melania actually smiled for the first time in four years. The real reason Trump is angry: Trudeau is everything Trump pretends to be—attractive, charming, competent, and genuinely liked. The jealousy was palpable. Also, the Barron rumors clearly bother him more than he admits. Note: This audition may have caused an international incident. Worth it.*

# Chapter 12
# Alec Baldwin's Audition

"Next audition is Alec Baldwin," Michelle announced.

Trump's face went through several emotions at once. "Baldwin? THE Baldwin? The guy who—"

"Yes. That Baldwin."

"Why would he audition? He hates me. He spent years mocking me on that stupid show."

"He submitted an application. A surprisingly sincere one, actually."

"What did it say?"

Michelle consulted her notes. "'I've spent so much time studying Trump's mannerisms that I probably know his body better than he does. Might as well put that to use.' End quote."

"That's not sincere, that's creepy."

"Nevertheless, he's next."

Trump crossed his arms. "Fine. But if he does that voice, I'm ending the audition immediately."

Alec Baldwin entered, looking remarkably normal—no wig, no orange makeup, just Baldwin in a well-fitted tuxedo. He shook Michelle's hand warmly.

"Mrs. Obama, thank you for having me."

"Mr. Baldwin. This should be... interesting."

Baldwin turned to Trump, extended his hand. Trump stared at it for a long moment before accepting.

"Donald," Baldwin said in his normal voice.

"Alec." Trump's tone could have frozen vodka.

"I appreciate the opportunity to audition."

"You spent four years making fun of me on national television."

"I spent four years playing you on national television. There's a difference."

"You made me look like an idiot."

"I made you look like you." Baldwin's smile was pleasant but sharp. "Shall we dance?"

They moved to the center of the floor. The pianist began a waltz. Trump assumed the lead position, jaw tight, clearly waiting for Baldwin to do something offensive.

Baldwin assumed the follower's position—and immediately began moving exactly as Trump moved. Not dancing with him, but mirroring him. Same posture, same stiffness, same awkward weight distribution.

Trump took a step. Baldwin took the exact same step, at the exact same time, in perfect synchronization.

"What are you doing?" Trump asked.

"Dancing." Baldwin's face had arranged itself into Trump's expression—that pursed-lip, suspicious look.

"You're copying me."

"I'm following your lead. That's how dancing works." But the mimicry was so precise it was uncanny.

They moved across the floor. Every time Trump shifted his weight, Baldwin shifted his weight. Every time Trump's hand tightened, Baldwin's hand tightened. It was like watching someone dance with their reflection.

Michelle made a note: *This is either genius or a war crime.*

"Stop it," Trump said.

"Stop what?" Baldwin's voice had shifted just slightly—not quite full Trump impression, but heading in that direction.

"That. What you're doing."

"I'm just dancing." The way he said "dancing"—the hand gesture, the facial expression—was pure Trump.

Trump tried a turn. Baldwin mirrored it perfectly, executing it in the exact same clumsy way Trump did, at the exact same time.

"You're mocking me!"

"I'm matching you. That's what a good partner does." Baldwin's posture was now completely Trump—the forward lean, the weird way Trump held his shoulders, even the angle of his head.

Trump stopped moving. Baldwin stopped moving at the exact same instant.

They stood frozen, facing each other, Trump staring at what looked like his own reflection in a fun house mirror.

"This is ridiculous," Trump said.

"This is ridiculous," Baldwin echoed, not quite perfectly synced, but close enough to be disturbing.

"Stop repeating me!"

"Stop repeating me!" Baldwin's timing was about a quarter-second off, like an echo.

Trump lunged forward. Baldwin lunged forward at the exact same moment. Their hands met in the middle.

"STOP!" Trump shouted.

Baldwin opened his mouth—and Trump actually flinched, waiting for the echo. But Baldwin just smiled and resumed his normal voice. "Sorry, I was just seeing if I still had it."

"Had what?"

"You. I played you for so long, your body language is burned into my brain. Every gesture, every tic, every unconscious movement. I know them better than you do."

"That's disturbing."

"That's method acting." Baldwin released Trump's hand, stepped back. "Should we actually dance now? Without the mirror routine?"

"I don't want to dance with you at all anymore."

"Come on, Donald. I came all this way. And I promise, no more mimicry." Baldwin extended his hand again. "Let me show you I can actually dance."

Trump hesitated, then took his hand. They assumed proper dance position.

The pianist restarted the waltz.

Baldwin danced—really danced. And he was good. Much better than Trump. Smooth, confident, leading effectively when he was supposed to follow, making Trump look almost competent through sheer technical skill.

But every so often—just for a split second—he'd slip. His face would do that Trump squint. His hand would make that Trump gesture. His posture would shift into that forward Trump lean.

Little flashes of Trump, like a light that couldn't quite stop flickering.

Trump noticed every single one. "You're doing it again!"

"Doing what?" Baldwin's face was innocent.

"The thing! The Trump thing!"

"I don't know what you're talking about." But his hand had just made the accordion gesture Trump always made when speaking.

"THERE! You just did it!"

"Did what?" Baldwin executed a perfect turn, but his facial expression during the turn was pure Trump—that satisfied look he got when he thought he'd said something clever.

Trump was getting flustered, missing steps, losing count. Baldwin remained smooth, making Trump look worse by comparison while periodically flashing these little moments of Trump mimicry.

"You know what your problem is?" Trump said. "You think you know me. You think playing me on TV means you understand me."

"I know you better than you know yourself." Baldwin's voice had shifted again, just slightly. "I've studied every speech, every interview, every hand gesture. I know what you're going to do before you do it."

"Prove it."

"Fine." Baldwin released Trump, stepped back. "Go ahead. Make any movement you want. Any gesture. I'll mirror it before you finish."

"That's impossible."

"Try me."

Trump raised his right hand slowly, pointing at Baldwin. Before his hand reached shoulder height, Baldwin's hand was already there, pointing back, the gesture identical down to the angle of his finger.

Trump tried a different move—the accordion hands. Baldwin's hands were already moving before Trump's started spreading apart.

Trump did the downward chopping motion he made when emphasizing a point. Baldwin's hand was already chopping before Trump's finished the movement.

"How are you doing that?" Trump demanded.

"Because I know you. I've lived inside your head for years. I know what you do when you're angry, what you do when you're defensive, what you do when you're lying—" he paused "—which is most of the time."

"That's enough!"

But Baldwin kept going, now doing a full Trump routine without music—the pointing, the accordion hands, the weird shoulder shimmy, the chin thrust, even the hair touch. It was like watching Trump's greatest hits performed by someone who'd studied them frame by frame.

"You walk like this—" Baldwin demonstrated Trump's forward-leaning walk.

"You talk like this—" The voice was now full Trump impression. "I'm going to do tremendous things, beautiful things, the best things anyone's ever seen—"

"STOP!" Trump was red-faced, actually backing away.

"You make this face when someone criticizes you—" Baldwin did the Trump defensive squint.

"And this face when you think you've won an argument—" The satisfied smirk was perfect.

"Michelle, make him stop!"

But Michelle was laughing—actually laughing, hand over her mouth, tears in her eyes. "I'm sorry, I can't—this is—" She couldn't finish the sentence.

Baldwin dropped the act, returned to his normal voice and posture. "See? I told you I knew you."

Trump was breathing hard, looking genuinely shaken. "You're not auditioning to be my dance partner. You're here to mock me."

"I'm here to show you what you look like from the outside. Consider it a public service."

"I don't need you to show me anything."

"Clearly you do, since you can't see how ridiculous you are." Baldwin straightened his bowtie. "Mrs. Obama, thank you for the opportunity. I think I've made my point."

He headed for the door, then paused. Without turning around, in perfect Trump voice: "This audition was tremendous. The best audition. Everyone's saying it."

After he left, Trump stood in the center of the East Room, still breathing hard, looking like someone who'd just seen a ghost.

"He's insane," Trump finally said. "Completely insane."

"He's very talented," Michelle corrected, wiping her eyes.

"He's a stalker! He studied me like a serial killer studies victims!"

"He's an actor who did his research. There's a difference."

Trump pulled out his phone, started typing furiously:

*Just had VERY STRANGE audition with Alec Baldwin (not funny!). He spent the whole time doing a bad impression of me instead of actually dancing. Very unprofessional! His career is over and everyone knows it. Sad to see someone so desperate for attention!*

He showed it to Michelle. "Good, right?"

"He's going to love that you proved his point by responding exactly how he knew you would."

"I'm not proving any—" Trump stopped. "Wait."

"He's in your head, Mr. President. The same way you're in his. The only difference is he's getting paid for it and winning Emmys."

Trump put his phone away without posting. Then took it out. Then put it away again. "I'm posting it."

"Of course you are."

"He can't just—he can't do that to me!"

"He already did. And you know what the worst part is?"

"What?"

"You're going to see that routine replayed on every late-night show for the next week. And each time you see it, you're going to get angrier, which will make you post more, which will make it a bigger story, which is exactly what he wants."

Trump stared at his phone. "I hate him."

"I know. He knows too. That's why this worked so well."

Michelle added a final note: *Baldwin—eliminated because he's too good at being Trump. Watching them together was like watching a man argue with his own reflection and lose. The mimicry was so precise it was almost cruel. Almost. Trump's rage means Baldwin succeeded perfectly. Will definitely watch the SNL sketch about this audition.*

# Chapter 13

# Supreme Leader Ali Khamenei's Audition

Michelle Obama stared at the audition application for a full minute before calling her assistant.

"Did you verify this?"

"Yes, ma'am. It came through official diplomatic channels. He's serious."

"The Supreme Leader of Iran wants to audition to be President Trump's dance partner."

"Apparently he's... curious about Western culture. His essay mentioned wanting to 'observe the decadence firsthand.'"

Michelle rubbed her temples. "Does the President know who's auditioning today?"

"We just told him 'a religious leader.' He seemed pleased."

"Oh no."

"Ma'am?"

"Nothing. Send him in."

Supreme Leader Ali Khamenei entered the East Room in full traditional dress—black robes, black turban, long white beard flowing down his chest. He moved with the dignity of someone who'd spent decades as Iran's highest authority. Two Iranian security personnel flanked him.

Trump bounded in from the opposite door, stopped, and beamed.

"Rabbi! Welcome!" He rushed forward with his hand extended. "Great to have you here! Which synagogue are you from? Brooklyn?"

Khamenei's expression didn't change, but something flickered in his eyes. He accepted the handshake slowly. "I am from Tehran."

"Tehran Street? Is that in Williamsburg? I know a lot of great people in Williamsburg. Very religious community. Very devoted."

"I am the Supreme Leader of the Islamic Republic of Iran."

Trump laughed, clapping Khamenei on the shoulder. "That's a good one! Islamic Republic! You rabbis have a great sense of humor. Very dry. I love it."

Michelle made a note: *This is happening. This is actually happening.*

"Mr. President," she said carefully, "perhaps we should clarify—"

"It's fine, Michelle. The rabbi and I are going to get along great." Trump turned back to Khamenei. "I love the outfit. Very traditional. Very authentic. My daughter Ivanka converted, you know. She's very observant. Keeps kosher, the whole thing."

Khamenei looked at his security detail. One of them whispered something in Farsi. Khamenei held up a hand—wait—and turned back to Trump with what might have been scientific curiosity.

"You believe I am a rabbi," Khamenei said slowly.

"Well, yeah. The beard, the hat, the black clothes. Very rabbinical. You look like you could be from my old neighborhood. We had a great rabbi when I was growing up. Rabbi Finklestein. You remind me of him."

"I see." Khamenei's voice was measured. "And you invited a rabbi to audition for your dance partner?"

"Why not? I love the Jewish community. Very supportive. Great dancers, too. I went to a bar mitzvah once—the hora, very energetic. Can you do the hora?"

"I... have not had occasion."

"We'll stick to the waltz then. More dignified anyway." Trump gestured to the pianist. "Shall we?"

Khamenei glanced at Michelle. She could only stare back, frozen between stopping this disaster and seeing where it went.

"Yes," Khamenei said finally. "We shall dance. For cultural... observation."

They moved to the center of the floor. Trump took Khamenei's hand, and they assumed dance position. The pianist began a waltz.

"So," Trump said as they started moving, "how's business at the synagogue? Good attendance?"

"The... synagogue. Yes. Very good attendance. Mandatory, one might say."

"That's great! Got to keep the community together. Very important. Do you do a lot of bar mitzvahs?"

"We have many ceremonies for young people, yes."

"Mazel tov! That's what you say, right? Mazel tov?"

"That is... one phrase that is used."

They continued dancing. Khamenei moved with surprising grace—he'd clearly been briefed on Western ballroom dancing. Trump, as usual, was competent but clumsy.

"You know," Trump said, "I've always supported Israel. Great country. Very strong. You must be very proud."

Khamenei's beard twitched slightly. "Proud."

"Of Israel. Your homeland."

"Ah. Yes. Israel. We have... strong feelings about Israel."

"See? I knew it! You rabbis are always very passionate about Israel. It's wonderful. I moved our embassy to Jerusalem. You probably loved that."

"It was... memorable."

One of Khamenei's security guards made a sound. The other elbowed him sharply.

Trump attempted a turn. Khamenei followed smoothly, his robes swirling.

"Nice moves! You're better than I expected. Do you dance at weddings? Jewish weddings always have the best dancing. Everyone gets up, very lively."

"Our weddings are quite... spirited, yes."

"And the food! I love kosher food. Had a great pastrami sandwich the other day. You keep kosher, right?"

"We have very strict dietary laws."

"Fantastic! No pork, I know that. Very healthy. I tried to cut pork out of my diet once, lasted about a week. Bacon got me." Trump laughed at his own joke.

Khamenei's expression remained unchanged. "Bacon is indeed ... problematic."

Michelle noticed that one of Khamenei's security guards was holding a small glass of something amber-colored. As she watched, Khamenei made a subtle gesture, and the guard set it on a nearby table. When Trump wasn't looking, Khamenei smoothly collected it and took a sip during a turn.

"Is that water?" Trump asked.

"For my throat. Very dry in Washington."

"Should we get you some tea? You rabbis love tea, right? With lemon?"

"This beverage is... sufficient." Khamenei took another sip. Michelle caught the scent—definitely not water. Definitely a mai tai.

They continued dancing. Trump was warming to his theme.

"You know what I love about the Jewish community? Very smart people. Very good with numbers. No offense, but it's true. Great businesspeople. I've done a lot of business with Jewish folks. Very sharp negotiators."

"We are... experienced in negotiation, yes."

"And the holidays! Hanukkah, Passover, Rosh Hashanah—I probably pronounced that wrong."

"Your pronunciation is... unique."

"I try. Ivanka taught me a lot. She's very knowledgeable. You should meet her sometime. She'd love to talk Torah with you."

Khamenei took another sip from his glass. "I would be... fascinated to discuss scripture with your daughter."

Trump attempted a dip. Khamenei went with it, surprisingly flexible, his beard nearly touching the floor.

"Wow! You're good at this! Must be all that davening. Builds core strength, right?"

"The daily prayers are indeed... physically demanding."

As Trump pulled Khamenei upright, one of the security guards refilled the glass and discretely passed it over. Khamenei accepted it without breaking stride.

"Is that your second drink?" Michelle asked.

"The spiritual leader requires... hydration." Khamenei's eyes were slightly brighter now. "The dancing is quite vigorous."

"Rabbi," Trump said, "I have to ask—what do you think of the ballroom project? Pretty impressive, right? The most beautiful ballroom ever built. I'm thinking of having a mezuzah installed. Would that be appropriate?"

Khamenei paused mid-step. "A mezuzah. In your ballroom."

"Yeah! Show respect for all religions. Very inclusive. Would you do the blessing thing?"

"I am not certain my particular... blessing style would be appropriate for a mezuzah."

"That's modest! I'm sure you're great at blessings. You're a spiritual leader! That's what you do!"

They danced in silence for a moment. Khamenei took another sip from his glass.

"This Western dancing," he said finally, "it is quite... intoxicating."

"Right? It's elegant! Classy! Much better than that hora stuff. No offense."

"None taken." Khamenei was definitely swaying slightly now. "Tell me, do all Western leaders dance with religious authorities?"

"Well, you're the first rabbi I've danced with. But I'm open-minded! I respect all religions. Well, most religions. Some are better than others. But Judaism, top tier. Really great religion."

"You are very... generous."

The music ended. Khamenei stepped back, slightly unsteady. His security guards immediately moved forward.

"That was great!" Trump said. "Really great! You're a strong candidate, Rabbi. Top five for sure. Maybe top three."

"I am... honored." Khamenei's English was getting slightly looser. "This has been most educational. Western decadence is exactly as I imagined."

"Decadence? This is just dancing! Wait till you see the grand opening. It's going to be spectacular! You should come! Bring the congregation!"

"The congregation. Yes. All eighty-five million of them."

"Big synagogue! Very impressive!"

One of the security guards whispered urgently to Khamenei in Farsi. Khamenei waved him off and turned back to Trump.

"Before I depart, I must ask—you are aware that last week you ordered military strikes against my... synagogue?"

Trump looked confused. "I did?"

"The nuclear facilities. In Tehran."

"Tehran the city? I thought you said Tehran Street!"

"I said I was from Tehran."

"Right, Tehran Street. In Brooklyn."

Khamenei stared at Trump for a long moment. Then he threw back his head and laughed—a genuine, slightly alcohol-enhanced laugh.

"You truly have no idea who I am."

"You're Rabbi... I'm sorry, I didn't catch your name."

"I am Ali Khamenei. Supreme Leader of Iran. You bombed my country."

Trump's face went through several expressions. "You're Iranian?"

"I thought the robes might have suggested this."

"I thought you were Hasidic!"

"I am Muslim. Very specifically Muslim."

"But the beard! The hat! The black clothes!"

"Many religious leaders dress this way. It is not exclusive to Judaism."

Trump turned to Michelle. "Did you know about this?"

"Yes, sir. I tried to tell you."

"You said 'a religious leader'!"

"I said THE religious leader. Of Iran. The country you bombed."

Trump looked back at Khamenei, who was finishing his third mai tai with evident satisfaction.

"So... you're not from Brooklyn?"

"I am from Mashhad originally. Though I have been in Tehran for many decades."

"And you came here to... to audition? After I bombed you?"

"I came to observe Western decadence firsthand. To understand the enemy. To see what kind of man orders strikes against my nation." Khamenei swayed slightly. "And to try these mai tais everyone speaks of. They are quite good."

"You're supposed to be our enemy!"

"Yes. And you are mine. Yet here we are, dancing. The universe has a sense of humor." Khamenei straightened his robes with dignity, despite the alcohol. "Thank you for the cultural experience, Mr. President. And for the excellent beverages. I now understand America much better."

"Wait, so you're really—you're actually—"

"The Supreme Leader of Iran. Yes. The man whose nuclear program you just bombed. That one."

"But we had a nice time!"

"We did. It was very strange. I will need to think about this." Khamenei headed for the door, his security guards supporting him slightly. At the threshold, he turned back. "Oh, and Mr. President? Next time you bomb a country, perhaps learn who leads it first."

"I knew who—I thought you were—but the beard—"

"Goodbye, Mr. President. Thank you for the dance. And the mai tais. Especially the mai tais."

After the Iranians left, Trump stood in the center of the East Room looking genuinely baffled.

"That wasn't a rabbi," he said finally.

"No, sir."

"That was the guy from Iran. The one on TV sometimes."

"Yes, sir."

"The one I bombed."

"Yes, sir."

"And I called him rabbi."

"Multiple times."

"And asked him about bar mitzvahs."

"And kosher food, and Israel, and mezuzahs."

Trump sat down heavily. "He's going to tell everyone, isn't he?"

"Oh, absolutely. This will be on Iranian state television within the hour."

"With the rabbi stuff?"

"Especially the rabbi stuff."

Trump pulled out his phone, stared at it, put it away. "I can't spin this. There's no spin for this."

"No, sir."

"I danced with Iran."

"You did."

"While thinking he was Jewish."

"Yes."

"And he was drinking on the job."

"He was drinking a lot on the job."

"Did he seem like he enjoyed it?"

Michelle considered this. "The mai tais or the dancing?"

"Both."

"Yes, sir. He seemed to thoroughly enjoy both."

Trump stood up, straightened his jacket. "Put him in the no pile."

"Obviously."

"But for the record—we danced pretty well together. Good rhythm. If he wasn't, you know, Iran, he'd be a strong candidate."

"I'll note that in my records."

"Don't note that in your records."

"Too late, sir."

After Trump left, Michelle added to her notes:

*Khamenei—eliminated because he is literally the Supreme Leader of a country we just bombed. The President spent the entire audition believing he was a rabbi from Brooklyn. When corrected, his response was essentially "but the beard!" Khamenei appeared to find this amusing, especially after three mai tais. This is either the beginning of an international incident or the most bizarre diplomacy in modern history. Possibly both. Note: The Supreme Leader of Iran has better dance skills than 80% of the people who've auditioned. Also note: The Supreme Leader of Iran can really put away mai tais. Most importantly: Never let the President plan foreign policy without a basic geography lesson.*

One of Khamenei's security guards had left his empty glass on the table. Michelle picked it up, sniffed it, and set it down.

"Well," she said to the empty room, "at least someone enjoyed themselves."

# Chapter 14
# Kristi Noem's Audition

Michelle Obama had seen beautiful women before. She'd met movie stars, supermodels, royalty. But Kristi Noem's face was something else entirely—a masterpiece of modern engineering that seemed to exist slightly outside the natural world.

The cheekbones were architectural. The lips were plump as throw pillows. The forehead was smoother than a frozen lake.

Nothing moved except what was supposed to move, and even that seemed to be on a slight delay.

"Mrs. Obama," Noem said, extending a hand. "Such an honor." Her smile engaged exactly the muscles required for smiling and nothing more.

"Governor—sorry, Secretary Noem," Michelle corrected herself. "Thank you for coming."

"Wouldn't miss it." Noem surveyed the East Room with the practiced eye of someone who'd spent years calculating camera angles. "Beautiful space. Very deportable lighting."

"I think you mean deportment. Or perhaps... suitable?"

"I know what I said." Noem winked. It took approximately two seconds longer than a natural wink.

Two Secret Service agents stood by the door. Noem walked over to them, reached into her Hermès bag, and produced two black tactical masks.

"Put these on," she said.

"Ma'am?" one agent asked.

"The masks. Put them on." She pressed them into their hands. "Makes me feel more at home."

The agents looked at each other, then at Michelle, who offered no guidance. They put on the masks.

"Much better," Noem said, returning to the center of the room. "Now it feels like a real government operation."

Trump entered, stopping short when he saw her. "Kristi! Wow. You look... you look incredible. Really incredible. What did you do? Something's different."

"Just freshened up a few things," Noem said. "New lips. New chin. Touched up the forehead. Added some volume here and there." She gestured vaguely at her entire face.

"Well, it's working. Very beautiful. Top three faces in the admin- istration, easily."

"Only top three?"

"Top two. Maybe top one. We'll see how the audition goes."

Michelle made a note: *This is what passes for flirtation in MAGA world.*

They moved to the center of the floor. The pianist began a foxtrot. Noem positioned herself in Trump's arms with practiced ease, camera-ready smile locked in place.

"You know," Trump said as they began to move, "I always thought you'd make a great dancer. Very graceful. Very elegant."

"I was Miss South Dakota Snow Queen," Noem said. "1990. We had a talent portion."

"I can tell. Natural performer."

They glided across the floor—Noem was, in fact, a competent dancer. Her body moved fluidly, even if her face remained suspiciously motionless.

"You're very stiff up top," Trump observed. "Relax your face a little."

"I can't, Mr. President. The Botox hasn't fully settled. My doctor said no major expressions for seventy-two hours."

"What happens if you make an expression?"

"We're about to find out." Noem attempted a laugh at something Trump whispered. There was a faint sound—something between a creak and a pop—from the region of her forehead.

"What was that?" Trump asked.

"Nothing. Minor adjustment." But a small bead of sweat had appeared at her hairline. "Keep dancing."

They continued. Michelle noticed that Noem's left eyebrow seemed slightly higher than it had been a moment ago. Then the right one began to rise to match.

"Your eyebrows are moving," Michelle observed.

"They're settling. It's normal."

"They're moving UP."

Noem's eyebrows continued their slow migration toward her hairline, giving her an expression of permanent, escalating surprise. She kept dancing as if nothing was happening.

"Should we stop?" Trump asked, staring at her forehead.

"Never stop for cosmetic adjustments, Mr. President. That's rule one in politics."

Trump attempted a turn. As Noem spun, something flew off her head—a long, black tendril that landed on the floor like a dead snake.

"What was that?" Trump jumped back.

"Hair extension. Don't worry, I have layers." She kept dancing, one hand casually reaching up to smooth over the gap. Another extension loosened, dangling precariously.

"You're falling apart," Trump said.

"I'm transitioning between looks. There's a difference."

They continued, Noem's face now locked in an expression of manic surprise, extensions dropping at irregular intervals. Trump stepped on one and stumbled slightly.

"Careful," Noem said. "That's Brazilian virgin hair. Three thousand dollars a bundle."

"It's on the FLOOR."

"It's still valuable."

Michelle watched, transfixed, as more extensions liberated themselves from Noem's scalp. The floor was beginning to look like a salon after closing.

But the real show was Noem's lips. They had begun to swell—slowly at first, then with gathering momentum. What had been "plump" was now approaching "inflatable."

"Your lips," Michelle said carefully. "They seem to be..."

"It's a delayed reaction," Noem said, her voice slightly muffled by the increasing volume of her own mouth. "Happens sometimes when my heart rate elevates. The filler migrates."

"Migrates WHERE?"

"Outward, mostly."

They kept dancing. Noem's lips continued to expand, now entering the realm of the genuinely alarming. They were approaching the size of small plums. Then tennis balls.

"This is concerning," Trump said, leaning back to avoid contact.

"It'll stabilize." Noem's voice was now almost incomprehensible, her massive lips interfering with consonants. "Juth keep danthing."

Trump attempted another turn. Noem spun, and her lips—now approaching the size of small grapefruits—swung outward with centrifugal force, catching Trump squarely on the neck.

"OW!" Trump grabbed his throat. "Your lips just hit me!"

"Thorry. Couldn't conthrole the momemtum."

"This is insane! You're a health hazard!"

"I'm a patrioth." The lips were still growing. "I'm jutht having a minor cothemtic event."

Michelle had stopped taking notes. She was simply staring, watching Noem's face transform into something from a medical textbook warning against discount procedures.

Trump backed away. "I think we're done here."

"But we haven't finithed the audithion!" Noem's lips were now genuinely grotesque, two glistening masses that seemed to have their own gravitational pull. Extensions littered the floor around her like the aftermath of a battle. Her eyebrows had nearly reached her hairline.

"You're not in any condition to—"

The East Room door burst open. A small dog—a Yorkshire terrier—came bounding in, yapping excitedly, trailing a leash. It belonged to the next audition candidate, who could be heard calling frantically from the hallway.

"Buttons! BUTTONS! Come back!"

The dog ran in circles, delighted by the new space, oblivious to the horror-show unfolding at its center.

Noem's expression—what could be read of it beneath the swelling—shifted. Her eyes tracked the dog with sudden, focused intensity.

"Excuthe me," she said, and walked toward the nearest masked Secret Service agent.

"Ma'am?"

"Your thidearm, pleath."

"Ma'am, I can't—"

"I'm the Thecretary of Homeland Thecurity. Give me your gun."

The agent, confused and alarmed, hesitated. Noem reached over, unholstered his weapon with practiced efficiency, turned, and aimed at the dog.

"NO!" Michelle shouted.

BANG.

Buttons the Yorkshire terrier dropped mid-yap.

Noem handed the gun back to the agent. "Thank you." She turned to Trump and Michelle, lips still massive, eyebrows still migrating, hair extensions still shedding. "Thorry about that. Re-flexth. Where were we?"

Silence. Absolute silence.

"I believe," Michelle said slowly, "we were finishing your audition."

"Did I path?"

"You just shot someone's dog."

"It wath a potential threath. I athessed the thituation and neu-tralithed it."

"It was a YORKSHIRE TERRIER."

"They can be vithiouth. I would know. I've thot dogth before."

Trump, for once in his life, seemed genuinely speechless.

From the hallway, a wail: "BUTTONS! BUUUUT-TOOOOONS!"

Noem straightened what remained of her hair, gathered some fallen extensions into her Hermès bag with dignity, and nodded to Michelle.

"Thank you for the opportunithy. I hope you'll conthider me for the firtht danthe. I bring a lot to the table—loyalty, dithipline, and a willingneth to do what needth to be done." She glanced at the dead dog. "Ath you can thee."

She walked out, lips leading the way like a ship's prow, stepping over a few fallen extensions, past the masked agents, past the sobbing dog owner in the hallway.

Trump finally found his voice. "She shot the dog."

"Yes."

"Just... shot it."

"Yes."

"During the audition."

"Yes."

"And her face..."

"Yes."

Trump pulled out his phone, then stopped. For once, he seemed unsure what to post.

"I don't..." he started. "That was..."

"Efficient," Michelle offered. "I believe she'd call it efficient."

"Her LIPS, Michelle. Her lips were the size of cantaloupes."

"I saw."

"And then she shot a dog. A tiny dog. Named Buttons."

"I was here, Mr. President."

Trump looked at the fallen Yorkie, the smattering of extensions, the masked Secret Service agents who seemed to be questioning every life choice that had led them to this moment.

"Put her in the maybe pile," he finally said.

"WHAT?"

"She's loyal. Very loyal. Decisive. I like decisive." He headed for the door, then turned back. "But maybe suggest she see a different cosmetic surgeon before the grand opening. The lip thing would be distracting on camera."

After he left, Michelle sat heavily in her chair. The dead dog was still on the floor. A staffer would have to deal with that. The extensions were the extensions. Another staffer problem.

She wrote in her notes: *Noem—demonstrated exactly who she is. Efficient, remorseless, and held together by foreign materials that are actively rebelling against her. Shot a dog named Buttons mid-audition without hesitation. Trump wants her in the maybe pile. I need a drink.*

# Chapter 15
# Little Johnny's Audition

Michelle Obama read the application essay one more time, smiling despite herself:

*My name is Johnny Martinez and I am 8 years old. My teacher Mrs. Patterson told us about the President's ballroom and how he needs a dance partner. I think I would be good because I learned the box step in PE and I am very responsible. Also my mom says I have good posture. I promise to behave and not touch anything expensive.*

*Thank you for your consideration. P.S. Susie says she should go in-stead but she can't even do a cartwheel so I think I am better.*

"This is adorable," Michelle said to her assistant. "But we can't actually—"

"The teacher submitted it as a class project. Said it would be educational."

"Educational for whom?"

"For the President, I imagine."

Michelle laughed. "Fine. Schedule him. This should be interesting."

Little Johnny arrived in a suit that was slightly too big, his hair combed neatly but already starting to stick up in places. He clutched a small backpack and stared around the East Room with wide eyes.

"Wow," he whispered. "This is SO cool."

"Johnny, I'm Michelle Obama. Thank you for coming."

"I know who you are! You're married to the other president!" Johnny shook her hand enthusiastically. "My mom voted for him. Both times."

"That's wonderful. Are you excited to dance with President Trump?"

"I guess. My dad says President Trump is a—" Johnny stopped, remembering his manners. "My dad says a lot of things about President Trump."

"I'm sure he does."

Trump entered, saw Johnny, and his face fell. "This is the audition? A kid?"

"An eight-year-old, sir. From Mrs. Patterson's third-grade class."

"I don't dance with kids. Kids are... sticky. And loud."

"Mr. President!" Johnny stepped forward. "I'm Johnny! I'm not sticky today. I washed my hands twice."

Trump looked at Michelle helplessly. "Can't we reschedule?"

"You have twenty minutes, sir. Let's make the best of it."

"Fine." Trump looked down at Johnny. "So. Kid. You think you can dance?"

"I learned the box step! Want to see?" Without waiting for an answer, Johnny began demonstrating, counting out loud. "One-two-three, one-two-three. See? My PE teacher Mr. Rodriguez says I'm a natural."

"That's... great." Trump checked his watch.

"Mr. President, you're really tall. Are you taller than my dad?"

"Probably. I'm six-three."

"My dad says you're five-eleven."

"Your dad is wrong."

"He says that a lot of times you're wrong, actually."

Michelle made a note: *This child is my hero.*

They moved to the center of the floor. The pianist began a simplified waltz. Johnny had to stand on a small platform to reach Trump's hands properly.

"Okay kid, I lead, you follow."

"Why do you get to lead?"

"Because I'm the president."

"So? I'm the third-grade representative to student council. That's basically the same thing."

"It's not—" Trump stopped himself. "Just follow, okay?"

They began to dance, if "dance" was the right word. Johnny was enthusiastic but erratic, occasionally forgetting the steps and improvising wildly.

"You're supposed to stay with the music," Trump said.

"I am with the music! I'm just adding my own style. That's called creative expression. Mrs. Patterson taught us about it."

"Well, Mrs. Patterson is wrong. Dancing has rules."

"Do you always follow rules?"

"That's different."

"How?"

"Because I'm an adult."

"My dad says you act like a kid sometimes."

Trump's jaw tightened. "Your dad talks a lot."

"Yeah, he really doesn't like you. He says—"

"Maybe we don't need to hear everything your dad says."

Johnny stepped on Trump's foot. "Oops! Sorry!"

"That's the third time."

"It's hard! Your feet are really big. Like clown feet."

"They're not clown feet!"

"Do you wear special shoes? My cousin has big feet and he has to order shoes from a catalog."

Michelle was writing so fast her hand was cramping.

"Can we just dance without talking?" Trump asked.

"But talking is fun! Don't you think talking is fun?"

"Not particularly."

"My mom says you talk too much on TV. She says you never stop talking. But now you don't want to talk to me?" Johnny looked genuinely confused.

"I talk about important things. Presidential things."

"Like what?"

"Like... policy. And the economy. And national security."

"What's national security?"

"It's—it's complicated."

"I'm eight, not dumb. Mrs. Patterson says we should always ask questions when we don't understand something."

Trump attempted a turn. Johnny spun with him but kept spinning after Trump stopped, got dizzy, and stumbled into a nearby chair.

"Are you okay?" Michelle rushed over.

"I'm fine! That was fun! Can we do it again?"

"Maybe let's stick to simpler moves," Trump said.

They resumed dancing. Johnny's backpack, which he'd insisted on keeping with him, kept swinging and hitting Trump's legs.

"What's in the backpack?" Trump asked.

"Stuff."

"What kind of stuff?"

"Important stuff."

"Can you take it off?"

"No, I might need it."

"Need it for what?"

"Emergencies." Johnny said this with complete seriousness.

Trump decided not to pursue it. They continued dancing, Johnny humming along with the music, occasionally breaking into spontaneous spins.

"Do you have any kids?" Johnny asked suddenly.

"Yes. Five."

"Do you dance with them?"

"Not really."

"Why not?"

"They're adults now. They don't want to dance with their father."

"That's sad. I dance with my dad sometimes. He's teaching me salsa." Johnny demonstrated a hip movement that was decidedly not waltz.

"That's not waltz."

"It's better than waltz! Waltz is boring."

"Waltz is elegant."

"Boring," Johnny repeated with confidence.

Trump looked at Michelle. "How much longer?"

"Fifteen more minutes, sir."

"Can't we just—"

"I need to go to the bathroom," Johnny announced.

"What?"

"Bathroom. You know, where you pee."

"I know what a bathroom is!"

"Then why did you say 'what'?"

"Because—never mind. Michelle, can someone take him to the bathroom?"

"There's one right through there." Michelle pointed.

"Don't touch anything!" Trump called as Johnny ran off, back-pack bouncing.

Trump stood alone in the center of the East Room, looking more rattled than he had after any previous audition. "Kids are the worst."

"He's eight years old and he's out-negotiating you."

"He is not—he's just talking a lot. Kids talk. It's what they do."

"He also called your feet 'clown feet' and you didn't have a comeback."

"I was being the bigger person. Literally. Because I'm much bigger. And older. And more important."

Johnny returned, drying his hands on his pants. "Your bath-rooms are really fancy! The soap smells like flowers!"

"Can we finish this?" Trump asked.

"Sure!" Johnny bounced back to the platform. "Wait, I almost forgot!" He dug into his backpack and pulled out a small plastic dinosaur. "This is Rex. He's a T-Rex. He's good luck."

"You brought a toy dinosaur to the White House?"

"He goes everywhere with me. Say hi to Rex!" Johnny held up the dinosaur.

Trump stared at the dinosaur. "Hi."

"You have to mean it. Rex can tell when people are being fake."

"I'm not being—fine. Hello, Rex. Nice to meet you."

"He says you seem stressed and should relax more."

"The dinosaur said that?"

"Yeah. He's very wise."

They resumed dancing, Rex now clutched in Johnny's left hand, occasionally bopping Trump's shoulder.

"Is the dinosaur going to hit me the whole time?" Trump asked.

"He's not hitting, he's keeping the beat!"

"That's not the beat."

"Rex says you're wrong."

Trump took a deep breath. "Four more minutes. I can do four more minutes."

"Mr. President," Johnny said, suddenly serious, "can I ask you something?"

"What?"

"Why do you want to build a ballroom?"

"Because it's important. For diplomacy and entertaining foreign leaders."

"But don't you have other places to do that?"

"Not nice enough."

"How much does it cost?"

"That's not your concern."

"My mom says it costs three hundred million dollars. That's a lot. We could build like, a million playgrounds with that."

"It's not about playgrounds."

"Why not? Kids like playgrounds."

"Because I'm not building things for kids. I'm building things for America."

"I'm America. I'm American."

Trump had no response to this.

The music ended. Johnny hopped off the platform and put Rex back in his backpack.

"That was fun! You're not as good at dancing as Mr. Rodriguez, but you're okay."

"Thanks," Trump said flatly.

"Mrs. Patterson is going to ask me what you're like. What should I tell her?"

"Tell her I'm tremendous. The best president ever."

Johnny tilted his head, considering. "My dad says you lie a lot. But you seem okay. You just don't know how to talk to kids. That's okay. My Uncle Steve is like that too. He gets all weird around me."

"I'm not weird around kids. I just don't—I'm very busy."

"Being president?"

"Yes."

"That sounds hard. Do you like it?"

The question seemed to catch Trump off guard. "I... it's very important. The most important job."

"That's not the same as liking it."

Trump looked at Johnny—really looked at him for the first time. "You're a weird kid."

"My mom says I'm perceptive. Is that the same thing?"

"Probably."

Johnny held out his hand. "Thank you for dancing with me, Mr. President. Even though you stepped on my foot twice and you don't listen very well."

Trump shook his hand. "You're welcome. Even though you called my feet clown feet and brought a dinosaur."

"Rex says goodbye." Johnny waved the dinosaur one more time, then headed for the door. He paused at the threshold. "Mr. President?"

"What?"

"You should dance with your kids sometime. Even if they're grown up. My dad says it's never too late to be a better person."

After Johnny left, Trump stood in the center of the East Room, looking genuinely thrown.

"That kid is going to be president someday," Michelle said.

"God help us."

"He asked better questions than most reporters."

"He asked annoying questions."

"He asked honest questions. There's a difference."

Trump pulled out his phone, stared at it, put it away. "I can't attack an eight-year-old on social media."

"That's very mature of you, sir."

"Even though he was very rude."

"He told you the truth. Children do that."

"Truth is overrated." Trump headed for the door. "Put him in the no pile."

"Obviously."

"But for the record—he wasn't the worst dancer."

"High praise coming from you, sir."

"Don't push it."

After Trump left, Michelle added to her notes:

*Little Johnny Martinez—eliminated because he's eight years old and has better sense than most of the adults who've auditioned. He called out the President's lies, questioned the ballroom's cost, suggested better uses for three hundred million dollars, and inadvertently gave Trump the best advice anyone's given him in years. Trump will ignore all of it. Johnny brought a toy dinosaur named Rex who was, according to Johnny, 'very wise.' Rex was correct to say Trump seemed stressed. Note: Johnny's father has excellent political instincts. Also note: If an eight-year-old can out-debate the President, we are in serious trouble. Most importantly: Johnny suggested Trump dance with his own children. The look on Trump's face suggested this had literally never occurred to him.*

She found a small plastic dinosaur sticker on the floor—Johnny must have dropped it. She picked it up and stuck it in her notebook.

"Thanks, Rex," she said to the empty room. "You tried."

# Chapter 16

# Justice Clarence Thomas's Audition

Michelle Obama was reviewing her notes when the East Room doors burst open. Justice Clarence Thomas rushed in, slightly out of breath, still wearing his black Supreme Court robes. He was fifteen minutes late.

"Mrs. Obama, my apologies. The oral arguments ran long, and I didn't have time to—"

Trump entered from the opposite door, saw Thomas, and immediately pointed.

"YOU!"

Thomas stopped. "Excuse me?"

"You think I'm stupid? You think I don't recognize you?" Trump strode forward, jabbing his finger. "You're that Iranian guy! The Ayatollah! Khamenei!"

Thomas blinked. "What?"

"Don't play dumb! The expression, the robes, the—you're sneaking back for more mai tais, aren't you?"

"Mr. President, I'm Justice Clarence Thomas. Of the Supreme Court. Of the United States."

"Nice try! That's exactly what you said last time! 'I'm from Tehran!' Well, I'm not falling for it again!"

Thomas looked at Michelle. "Is he serious?"

"I'm afraid so, sir."

"Mr. President," Thomas said slowly, "I am a Supreme Court Justice. I have been on the Court since 1991. I was appointed by George H.W. Bush. I am not Iranian. I am from Pin Point, Georgia."

"Pin Point? Is that near Tehran Street?"

Thomas closed his eyes briefly. "It's in Georgia. The state. In America."

"That's what you'd say if you were trying to trick me!"

"Why would the Supreme Leader of Iran pretend to be a Supreme Court Justice?"

"For the mai tais! Obviously!" Trump looked around. "Where are they? Did you hide them already?"

Michelle intervened. "Mr. President, this is actually Justice Thomas. He's here for his scheduled audition. He came straight from the Court, which is why he's wearing his robes."

Trump squinted at Thomas. "How do I know this isn't a trick?"

"Because I voted to give you full immunity from prosecution," Thomas said flatly. "In Trump v. United States. July 2024. Six to three decision."

"You did?"

"Yes."

"Really?"

"Unfortunately, yes."

Trump's expression changed. "Oh! You're the Supreme Court guy! The conservative one!"

"That's one way of putting it."

"Why didn't you say so?"

"I did. Multiple times. In the last ninety seconds."

Trump waved this off. "Well, you should have been clearer. You look just like that Iranian guy."

"I look nothing like the Supreme Leader of Iran."

"The expression, the robes—"

"His robes are brown. Mine are black. His turban is black. I'm not wearing a turban. We look completely different."

"If you say so." Trump was already moving past it. "So you're here to dance?"

Thomas took a deep breath. "Yes. That's why I submitted an audition application. That's why I'm here. That's why I rushed from oral arguments without changing."

"Great! Let's dance!" Trump seemed genuinely pleased now. "You gave me immunity! That's tremendous! Really tremendous! You're one of the good ones!"

"I'm reconsidering that assessment," Thomas muttered.

They moved to the center of the floor. Thomas was still adjusting his robes, which were not designed for ballroom dancing.

"Should I take these off?" Thomas asked.

"No, keep them! Very impressive! Very official!" Trump was in a good mood now. "You're the guy who likes RVs, right?"

Thomas's expression froze. "I'm sorry?"

"The RV thing. I read about it. Some guy bought you an RV?"

"That was... a gift. From a friend."

"Must be a good friend! Those things are expensive!"

"Mr. President, perhaps we should focus on the dancing?"

"And the yacht trips! Someone said you take yacht trips!"

"Those were disclosed appropriately."

"Must be nice! Who's the friend? Can I meet him? I like people who give expensive gifts!"

The pianist began a waltz. They assumed dance position, Thomas's robes swishing around their feet.

"You're very quiet usually, right?" Trump asked as they began to move. "I heard you never talk during the arguments."

"I prefer to listen."

"That's weird. I prefer to talk. Talking is how you show you're smart."

"Or you could show it through your decisions."

"But then people don't know you're smart right away. You have to make sure people know immediately."

They danced in silence for a moment. Thomas was competent but clearly uncomfortable in his robes.

"So," Trump said, "the immunity thing. That was huge for me. Really huge. You basically said I can do whatever I want, right?"

"That's not exactly what the decision said."

"But close enough, right? Presidential immunity?"

"The decision was more nuanced than—"

"Nuance is boring. The point is, I'm immune. That's tremendous. You did a great job on that."

Thomas's jaw tightened. "I'm glad you're pleased."

"I am pleased! Very pleased! You should do more things like that!"

"More things like... giving presidents immunity from prosecution?"

"Yeah! Make the presidency stronger! More powerful! I have so many great ideas but people keep saying I can't do them because of laws or whatever."

"Those laws are the Constitution."

"Details!" Trump attempted a turn, nearly tripping on Thomas's robes. "Watch the dress!"

"These are judicial robes, not a dress."

"Whatever they are, they're a tripping hazard."

They continued dancing, Trump increasingly animated, Thomas increasingly quiet.

"You know what else you should do?" Trump said. "That affirmative action thing you got rid of. That was great! Really great!"

"The Students for Fair Admissions decision."

"Yeah! No more special treatment! Everyone should be treated the same!"

Thomas stopped dancing. "Mr. President, do you understand the irony of you praising that decision?"

"What irony?"

"Never mind."

"No, what? Tell me."

"It's nothing."

"You're doing that quiet thing again. The brooding thing. Just say what you're thinking."

Thomas looked at Trump for a long moment. "I was thinking that I spent my entire career arguing that people should be judged on merit, not circumstances. And then I gave immunity to someone who's never achieved anything on merit in his entire life."

"Hey!"

"You were born rich. You inherited hundreds of millions. You've failed upward your entire life. And I protected you from consequences." Thomas's voice was quiet but intense. "I've been thinking about that a lot lately."

"I earned everything I have!"

"You declared bankruptcy six times."

"That's just smart business!"

"You were found liable for sexual assault."

"That was a rigged trial!"

"You incited an insurrection."

"That's fake news!"

"And I gave you immunity." Thomas stepped back. "What was I thinking?"

Trump's face was red. "You're supposed to be on my side!"

"I'm supposed to be on the Constitution's side. But lately, I'm not sure what side I'm on anymore."

They had stopped dancing entirely. Thomas's robes hung heavy around him, suddenly looking less like symbols of authority and more like the weight of his decisions.

"You know what your problem is?" Trump said. "You think too much. That's why you never talk during arguments. You're overthinking everything."

"Perhaps. Or perhaps I'm finally thinking clearly for the first time in years."

"What's that supposed to mean?"

Thomas looked around the East Room—the chandeliers, the portraits, the history. "It means maybe I shouldn't be here. Maybe none of us should be here. Maybe we've all lost sight of what we're supposed to be doing."

"We're dancing! We're supposed to be dancing!"

"No, Mr. President. We're supposed to be governing. We're supposed to be serving the American people. We're supposed to be upholding the Constitution. But instead, you're building a three-hundred-million-dollar ballroom, and I'm—" He stopped. "I'm dancing with you in my robes while people question whether I should even be on the Court."

"Nobody's questioning—"

"Everyone's questioning. The gifts, the trips, the decisions. And you know what? They should be. I should be questioned. Because somewhere along the way, I forgot that being on the Supreme Court isn't about loyalty to a party or a president. It's about the law."

Trump pointed at him. "You're having a breakdown. That's what this is. A judicial breakdown."

"Maybe. Or maybe I'm having a moment of clarity." Thomas began removing his robes, revealing a simple suit underneath. "Mrs. Obama, I apologize, but I need to leave."

"Justice Thomas, are you alright?"

"I'm not sure. I need to think. I need to—" He looked at his robes in his hands. "I need to figure out if I can still wear these with integrity."

"You're being dramatic," Trump said. "It's all that thinking! That's what thinking does! Makes you dramatic!"

Thomas folded his robes carefully. "Mr. President, thank you for the dance. And thank you for the reminder."

"Reminder of what?"

"Of why I need to be more careful about my decisions. Both on the Court and off it."

He walked to the door. At the threshold, he turned back.

"Oh, and Mr. President? That immunity decision? If I could take it back, I would. But I can't. So I'll have to live with it. We all will."

After he left, Trump stood confused. "What just happened?"

"I believe Justice Thomas had an existential crisis, sir."

"A what?"

"He questioned his life choices."

"Because of dancing?"

"Because of you, sir. You have that effect on people."

Trump pulled out his phone, started typing, stopped. "What do I even say about that?"

"Perhaps nothing would be best."

"But he was weird! Very weird! Started talking about the Constitution and integrity and—"

"Sir, the man is on the Supreme Court. Those are literally his job responsibilities."

"He should have thought about that before he gave me immunity!"

"I believe that's exactly what he was thinking about."

Trump pocketed his phone, shaking his head. "Put him in the no pile."

"With pleasure, sir."

After Trump left, Michelle added to her notes:

*Justice Thomas—eliminated because he arrived late, was mistaken for the Supreme Leader of Iran, and had an apparent crisis of conscience about giving Trump immunity from prosecution. The moment he said "I voted to give THIS guy full immunity?" with genuine regret was possibly the most honest thing any Trump appointee has said in years. Note: Thomas removed his robes mid-audition, which feels symbolic of something but I'm too tired to figure out what. Most importantly: If a Supreme Court Justice can have a moment of moral clarity while waltzing with Trump, there might be hope for this country yet. But probably not.*

She noticed Thomas had left his robes draped over a chair. She picked them up, folded them more neatly, and set them aside.

"Good luck with your thinking, Justice Thomas," she said to the empty room. "You're going to need it."

# Chapter 17

# Karoline Leavitt's Audition

Michelle Obama had developed a sixth sense for when an audition would be uncomfortable. The moment she saw Trump arrive twenty minutes early, checking his hair in every reflective surface, she knew this would be worse than uncomfortable.

"Who's auditioning today?" Trump asked, trying to sound casual.

"Karoline Leavitt."

"Oh. Good. She's very professional. Very good at her job." He adjusted his tie for the third time. "What time did you say she was coming?"

"2 PM."

"And it's..." He checked his watch. "1:40. So I have time to—I should probably—does my hair look okay?"

"Your hair looks exactly like it always looks, Mr. President."

"Right. Good. That's good." He sat down, stood up, sat down again. "Karoline's very dedicated. Very loyal. Did I mention she's good at her job?"

"You did, sir."

At precisely 2 PM, Karoline Leavitt entered wearing a purple dress that was somehow both appropriate for the White House and completely inappropriate for a professional setting. Her signature oversized gold cross hung prominently around her neck, swinging slightly as she walked. Her hair was perfect, her makeup was perfect, and her lips—Michelle noticed Trump's eyes immediately fix on them—were glossed to an almost reflective sheen.

"Mr. President!" Leavitt's voice was bright, breathy. "This is so exciting!"

"Karoline! You look—you look very professional. Very appropriate." Trump was standing now, smoothing his jacket. "Great cross. Very religious. I love that about you."

"Thank you, sir. My husband gave it to me." She touched the cross, making it catch the light.

"Your husband. Right. How is—what's his name again?"

"Nicholas. He's wonderful. Very supportive of my career."

"That's great. Really great. How old is Richard, I mean Nicholas, now?"

"Sixty, sir."

"Sixty. Wow. That's... that's really..." Trump seemed to lose his train of thought, staring at her lips.

Michelle made a note: *I need to shower after this.*

They moved to the center of the floor. The pianist began a waltz. Trump and Leavitt assumed dance position, standing closer than was strictly necessary.

"You smell nice," Trump said.

"Thank you, sir. It's Chanel."

"Very classy. Very expensive."

"Nicholas likes me to smell nice."

"Richard, I mean Nicholas, has good taste." Trump's eyes were still fixed on her mouth. "Your lipstick is a nice color."

"Do you think so? I tried three different shades this morning."

"It's perfect. Really perfect. Very... moist."

Michelle's pen nearly tore through the paper.

They began to dance. Leavitt was competent—she'd clearly taken lessons recently—and she gazed up at Trump with the expression of someone who'd perfected adoration as a professional skill.

"You know," Trump said, "you do a great job at those press conferences. Really great. Very attractive—I mean, effective. Very effective."

"I learned from the best, sir. You."

"I am pretty good at press conferences."

"The best. When you speak, I just hang on every word." She was practically purring.

"That's because you're smart. Beautiful AND smart."

"Mr. President, you're going to make me blush."

"You look great when you blush. That lip color really—I mean, you have very expressive features."

They continued dancing, Trump pulling her incrementally closer with each turn. Leavitt didn't resist. The cross swung between them like a pendulum.

"That's a very large cross," Michelle observed.

"I wear it at all my press briefings," Leavitt said. "It reminds me to speak the truth."

Michelle made a note: *The lies she tells while wearing that cross could fill the Library of Congress.*

"It's beautiful," Trump said. "Very beautiful. Like everything about you. Your dedication, your loyalty, your..." His eyes dropped to her lips again. "Your commitment to the job."

"I'm committed to YOU, sir."

"That's what I like to hear."

Michelle stood up. "Perhaps we should try something more complex. A dip, maybe?"

"A dip!" Trump's face lit up. "Great idea. Karoline, have you ever been dipped?"

"Not by a president." Was she actually batting her eyelashes?

"Well, you're in for a treat. I'm very good at dips."

They positioned themselves. Trump counted down. "On three. One... two... THREE!"

He leaned Leavitt backward. She went easily, practiced, that cross swinging forward with momentum. Trump dipped her lower, lower, trying to impress her with his strength and control.

The cross, following the laws of physics, swung up toward Leavitt's face.

It happened in slow motion: the heavy gold cross arcing upward, Leavitt's mouth opening slightly in surprise, Trump leaning further to make the dip more dramatic.

The cross flew directly into her open mouth.

Leavitt made a sound—"GLRK!"—and her eyes went wide.

Trump pulled her upright. "Are you okay? Did you bite your tongue? Your lips okay?"

Leavitt was making choking sounds, hands at her throat. The chain had broken, and the cross was lodged somewhere in her airway.

"Oh my god," Michelle said, already moving toward her. "She's choking!"

"Her lips!" Trump said. "Are her lips okay?"

"Mr. President, she's CHOKING ON HER CROSS!"

"But her mouth—did she damage her mouth?"

Leavitt's face was turning red. She was pointing at her throat, still making horrible gagging sounds.

Michelle grabbed the phone on the wall. "I need the White House Emergency Medical Team in the East Room. NOW!"

"Check her lips first!" Trump was hovering around Leavitt like an agitated hummingbird. "Make sure nothing's bleeding!"

"Mr. President, she is literally choking to death!"

"But if her lips are damaged—"

A young man burst through the door, barely twenty-two, wearing scrubs that looked like they'd been borrowed from a costume shop. He was breathing hard, carrying a first aid kit that appeared to contain mostly band-aids.

"I'm here!" he announced. "I'm the medical team!"

"Where is everyone else?" Michelle demanded.

"DOGE eliminated the positions. It's just me now. I'm Brad. I'm an intern. Well, I was pre-med for one semester before I switched to communications, but I watched a YouTube video on the Heimlich last week."

Leavitt's face was now approaching purple.

"DO SOMETHING!" Michelle shouted.

"Right! Okay!" Brad dropped his first aid kit, which spilled band-aids everywhere. "So I get behind her and—where do my hands go again?"

"JUST BELOW THE RIBCAGE!"

"Her lips," Trump kept saying, circling them. "Save the lips. Please save the lips."

"Mr. President, she needs to BREATHE!"

"She can breathe through her nose if her lips aren't damaged!"

Brad got behind Leavitt, wrapped his arms around her, and squeezed. Nothing happened.

"Higher!" Michelle instructed.

Brad adjusted, squeezed again. Still nothing.

Leavitt was now making no sound at all, her eyes rolling back.

"HARDER!" Michelle yelled.

"The lips!" Trump shouted. "BE CAREFUL OF THE LIPS!"

Brad squeezed with all his strength. There was a horrible retching sound, and the gold cross flew out of Leavitt's mouth, trailing saliva, and landed on the floor with a clunk.

Leavitt gasped, coughed, doubled over, gasping in huge lungfuls of air.

"Her lips!" Trump immediately crouched down next to her. "Let me see. Open your mouth. Are they okay?"

Leavitt was still coughing, tears streaming down her face.

"Sir, give her space!" Michelle pushed him back.

Brad stood there, hands still in Heimlich position, looking shocked. "Did I do it? Did I save her?"

"Yes, you saved her! Now get her some water!"

"We have water?"

"THE SINK! USE THE SINK!"

Brad ran off in search of water.

Trump was still fixated on Leavitt. "Your lips look okay. Maybe a little swollen. But mostly okay. That's good. Really good. I was worried."

Leavitt, finally able to speak, whispered hoarsely, "Thank you... Mr. President... for caring... about my lips."

"Of course I care! They're very important lips! National security depends on those lips!"

"That's not how national security works!" Michelle said.

Brad returned with water in a coffee mug. Leavitt drank, still coughing occasionally, her perfect hair now disheveled, her make-up smeared, but miraculously alive.

"So," Trump said after a moment, "does this mean we're done with the audition?"

"YES!" Michelle said. "Very much yes!"

"But we didn't finish the dance."

"She nearly died, Mr. President!"

"But she didn't! She's fine! Look, her lips are already returning to normal color."

Leavitt managed a weak smile. "I'm okay, sir. Really. Just... need a minute."

"Take all the time you need." Trump patted her shoulder awkwardly. "Your dedication is incredible. Nearly dying and still committed to the audition. That's loyalty."

Michelle added to her notes with shaking hands:

*Leavitt—eliminated due to near-death experience. The President's concern for her lips over her life was disturbing but entirely predictable. The cross was a choking hazard waiting to happen. The DOGE cuts to medical staff nearly resulted in a fatality. Brad the intern somehow succeeded despite having no qualifications whatsoever. Note: When Trump said 'national security depends on those lips,' I briefly considered quitting. Leavitt's willingness to continue the audition after nearly dying suggests either incredible dedication or a complete lack of self-preservation instinct. Possibly both. The cross is currently evidence in what should be an OSHA investigation that will never happen.*

Trump helped Leavitt to a chair, still fussing over her. "You should go home, rest. Take tomorrow off from press briefings."

"No sir, I'll be there. The American people need to hear from you."

"Through you. Through your very important lips."

"Yes sir."

Michelle closed her portfolio. "Brad, please escort Ms. Leavitt to her office and make sure she's okay."

"Yes ma'am!" Brad was just happy to have successfully completed a medical procedure.

After they left, Trump picked up the cross from the floor. "Should we save this? Maybe as a reminder of her dedication?"

"Put it down, sir."

"It's evidence of loyalty. Nearly died while wearing a cross, serving her president."

"It's evidence that your ballroom project is a health hazard."

Trump pocketed the cross. "I'll return it to her. Maybe have it bronzed or something. 'The cross that survived.'"

"That's macabre."

"That's memorable." He headed for the door. "Put her in the strong maybe pile."

"She nearly DIED!"

"But she didn't. And she wanted to keep dancing. That's the kind of commitment I need in a dance partner."

After he left, Michelle sat alone in the East Room. The broken chain was still on the floor. Band-aids were scattered everywhere. There was a small pool of water where Brad had spilled the coffee mug.

She pulled out her phone and texted her husband: *I need a vacation. Also, we need to talk about the state of White House medical coverage. Love you.*

The response came quickly: *Love you too. How bad was today?*

Michelle looked around the East Room—the scene of what could have been a tragedy, saved only by a marginally competent intern and sheer dumb luck.

*On a scale of one to ten? Eleven.*

# Chapter 18
# Kash Patel's Audition

Michelle Obama had read Kash Patel's file three times and still wasn't sure he was a real person. Former public defender turned conspiracy theorist turned Trump loyalist turned FBI Director. The trajectory didn't make sense, but then again, nothing about this administration made sense.

Patel entered the East Room with the energy of someone who believed he was on a secret mission. He walked with purpose, head slightly forward, and those eyes—Michelle had seen the photos, but they were more intense in person. Wide, unblinking, with an almost hypnotic quality.

"Mrs. Obama," he said, extending his hand. His handshake lasted exactly three seconds too long. "It's an honor to participate in this crucial selection process."

"Mr. Director, thank you for coming."

"Please, call me Kash. We're all on the same team here. Well, most of us." He glanced around the room as if checking for surveillance devices. "The ballroom project is strategically important. Very important. Some people don't understand how important, but I do."

"It's... a dance audition."

"Is it though?" Patel's eyes widened slightly. "Or is it something more?"

Before Michelle could respond, Trump entered.

"Kash!" Trump seemed genuinely pleased. "Good to see you. You're doing great work at the FBI. Really cleaning house."

"Thank you, Mr. President. I'm honored to—"

"Yeah, yeah, let's dance. Michelle says you can dance. Can you dance?"

"I can do whatever needs to be done, sir." Patel's eyes locked onto Trump's. "Whatever you need."

They moved to the center of the floor. The pianist began a waltz. Trump and Patel assumed dance position, and something immediately felt off to Michelle. The way Patel was looking at Trump—those wide, unblinking eyes—seemed to have a strange effect.

Trump's posture relaxed. His usual aggressive energy softened.

"You know, Kash," Trump said dreamily, "you're one of my best appointments. Really tremendous."

"Thank you, sir." Patel's eyes never wavered. "I'm here to serve."

They began to dance. Patel wasn't particularly skilled, but something about the way he moved—smooth, steady, hypnotic—made Trump follow without his usual resistance.

"The deep state is real," Patel said softly. It wasn't a question, just a statement.

"The deep state is real," Trump echoed, his voice oddly monotone.

Michelle's pen paused over her notebook. *What is happening?*

"They're everywhere, Mr. President. In the agencies, in the courts, in the—"

"Everywhere," Trump repeated. His eyes had gone slightly glassy.

"We need to root them out. All of them."

"All of them." Trump nodded slowly, moving in perfect sync with Patel now.

Patel's eyes seemed to grow wider, more intense. "You trust me, don't you, Mr. President?"

"I trust you, Kash."

"You know I only want what's best for you."

"Only what's best."

They were moving in an unnaturally synchronized way now, like two parts of the same mechanism. Patel led, but it wasn't traditional leading—it was something else. Something that made Michelle deeply uncomfortable.

"Mr. President," she said loudly, trying to break whatever was happening.

Trump didn't respond. He was staring into Patel's eyes.

"The election was stolen," Patel said.

"The election was stolen," Trump repeated.

"Everyone knows it."

"Everyone knows it."

"Mr. President!" Michelle said more forcefully.

Trump blinked, shook his head slightly. "What? Sorry, I was—Kash, what were we talking about?"

"Just dancing, sir." Patel's smile was pleasant, but those eyes remained fixed on Trump's face.

Trump looked back at him. Within seconds, the glazed expression returned.

"You should give me more authority," Patel said softly.

"More authority," Trump echoed.

"Unlimited access. To everything."

"Everything." Trump's voice was dreamy again.

"The FBI needs to investigate your enemies."

"My enemies."

"All of them. Starting with—"

"OKAY!" Michelle stood up. "I think we need to take a break."

Patel finally looked away from Trump, turning those intense eyes on Michelle. She felt a strange pull, a desire to just sit back down and let whatever was happening continue.

She shook her head sharply. *No. Absolutely not.*

Trump stumbled slightly, as if released from strings. "What—did I just—Kash, was I talking?"

"Just about the usual things, sir. The deep state. Your enemies. The stolen election."

"I say that all the time anyway." Trump rubbed his eyes. "Why do I feel weird?"

"Perhaps you're tired, Mr. President." Patel's voice was soothing. "You work so hard. Too hard."

"I do work hard." Trump looked at Patel again. The glazed expression started to return.

Michelle physically stepped between them. "Mr. Director, I think that's enough for today."

"But we haven't finished the audition."

"Oh, I think we have."

Patel smiled, those eyes sliding past Michelle to find Trump again. "Mr. President, I hope you'll consider me seriously for the first dance. I think we work very well together. Very... synchronized."

"We do," Trump said distantly. "Very synchronized."

"Mr. President," Michelle said sharply, snapping her fingers near his face. "Focus on me."

Trump blinked, shook his head again. "Sorry, I keep—what's wrong with me?"

"Nothing's wrong, sir," Patel said. "You're just recognizing the truth. We understand each other. We see things the same way."

"The same way," Trump repeated.

"OKAY, WE'RE DONE!" Michelle physically took Trump's arm and pulled him away from Patel. "Thank you for coming, Director Patel. We'll be in touch."

"Of course, Mrs. Obama." Patel adjusted his tie, those eyes still locked on Trump. "Mr. President, remember what we discussed. The deep state. Your enemies. My authority."

"I remember." Trump's voice was foggy.

"You'll make the right decisions."

"The right decisions."

"Director Patel," Michelle said firmly, "please leave. Now."

Patel finally broke eye contact with Trump. He nodded to Michelle, gathered his things, and walked to the door. At the threshold, he turned back.

"Mr. President?"

Trump automatically looked at him.

"I'll see you at the security briefing tomorrow. We have much to discuss."

"Much to discuss," Trump echoed.

After Patel left, Michelle made Trump sit down and brought him a glass of water.

"Drink this. Don't talk, just drink."

Trump drank, his eyes gradually clearing. "What just happened?"

"I'm not entirely sure, but it was deeply concerning."

"I kept saying things. Things I believe, but I don't usually say them like that. Like I was..."

"Hypnotized?"

"That's crazy. You can't hypnotize someone just by looking at them."

"Apparently Kash Patel can." Michelle reviewed her notes. "Mr. President, during that audition, you agreed to give him unlimited authority, to investigate all your enemies, and you repeated every single conspiracy theory he mentioned without question."

"I did?"

"Verbatim. Like you were under some kind of spell."

Trump pulled out his phone, started to post something, then stopped. "What should I post about him?"

"Nothing. Don't engage. Don't look at photos of him. Don't think about him."

"Why not?"

"Because I'm genuinely concerned that man has some kind of... I don't know what to call it. Influence. And not the normal kind."

Trump stared at his phone. "He's a great FBI Director though. Really loyal."

"That's exactly what I'm worried about."

"Maybe I should give him more authority."

"Mr. President—"

"What? He's doing a great job cleaning out the deep state."

Michelle closed her portfolio with a sharp snap. "And there it is. He's still in your head."

"He's not in my head. I just think he makes good points about—"

"Stop. Right now. We're not discussing Kash Patel anymore."

Trump looked confused, then annoyed. "Fine. But he's definitely in the running for the dance partner."

"Absolutely not."

"Why not? We synchronized well."

"You synchronized TOO well. That's the problem."

"You're being paranoid."

"One of us needs to be." Michelle stood, gathered her things. "Next audition is tomorrow. I'm choosing someone completely different. Someone normal."

"Who?"

"I haven't decided yet, but they will not have hypnotic eyes."

After Michelle left, Trump sat alone in the East Room. He pulled out his phone, started scrolling, and found a photo of Kash Patel from a recent press conference.

Those eyes stared out from the screen.

Trump stared back.

For a long moment, nothing happened.

Then Trump heard himself say, quietly, "I should give Kash more authority."

He shook his head sharply, put the phone away. Pulled it out again. Looked at the photo.

"More authority," he whispered.

His phone rang—a staffer with a question about the schedule. The spell broke.

Trump looked at his phone one more time, then turned it face-down on the table.

"That's crazy," he said to the empty room. "You can't hypnotize people through photographs."

But he didn't look at the phone again.

Michelle, reviewing her notes in her office, added a final entry:

*Patel—absolutely eliminated. Not because he can't dance (he can't), but because he has some kind of unnatural influence over the President. Possibly hypnosis, possibly just extreme cult-of-personality dynamics, possibly something I don't have a word for. Whatever it is, watching Trump turn into a compliant zombie while staring into Patel's eyes was the most disturbing audition yet. Note: Recommend President avoid direct eye contact with FBI Director. Also recommend getting Patel a psychological evaluation. Also recommend getting TRUMP a psychological evaluation. Also recommend updating my resume.*

# Chapter 19
# Claudia Sheinbaum's Audition

Michelle Obama heard the mariachi band before she saw it. Five musicians in full charro outfits had somehow been installed in the corner of the East Room, instruments at the ready, looking confused about why they were there.

"What is happening?" Michelle asked the nearest Secret Service agent.

"The President requested them, ma'am. For the Mexican president's audition."

"Oh no."

"There's more, ma'am."

"Of course there is."

Trump burst through the doors wearing an enormous sombrero—the kind sold at tourist shops in Cancún, decorated with "MEXICO" embroidered in rainbow thread. He carried a large paper bag with "José's Taco Shack" printed on the side.

"Michelle! Perfect timing! I brought authentic Mexican food!" He set the bag on a side table. "Real tacos. Not that Taco Bell garbage. These are from José."

"Mr. President, why are you wearing that hat?"

"To show respect! Claudia's Mexican. This is Mexican. It's cultural diplomacy." He adjusted the sombrero, which was comically oversized. "And I got the band. Real mariachis. Nothing but the best."

"Sir, President Sheinbaum is—"

"A very impressive woman. Very impressive. Smart, tough, good-looking—I mean, professional-looking. I want her to know I respect her culture."

The doors opened. Claudia Sheinbaum entered in a simple, elegant black pantsuit. She had a PhD in energy engineering, had been mayor of Mexico City, and carried herself with the confidence of someone who'd never doubted her competence. She looked at Trump's sombrero.

Her expression didn't change, but something flickered in her eyes.

"Presidente Trump," she said, her English perfect and unaccented.

"Presidente Sheinbaum!" Trump beamed. "Welcome! Bien-venidos! I brought tacos!" He gestured at the bag like he was presenting a diplomatic gift.

"How... thoughtful." She glanced at Michelle. "Mrs. Obama, a pleasure to see you again."

"President Sheinbaum, thank you for coming. Please ignore the—" Michelle gestured vaguely at everything "—theatrics."

"I've learned to expect them."

Trump grabbed the taco bag. "Here, try one! They're authentic! José makes them himself!"

"I have eaten tacos before, Presidente Trump. I am from Mexico."

"Right, right, but these are really good ones. José is—well, I assume he's Mexican. He has the mustache."

Sheinbaum's eyebrow raised approximately one millimeter. "I see."

Trump set down the bag, suddenly uncertain. "I thought you'd appreciate—I mean, it's your culture—"

"Presidente Trump, I am from Mexico City. I have a PhD in energy engineering from UNAM and a master's from UC Berkeley. My culture is not adequately represented by a bag of tacos from 'José's Taco Shack.'"

"No, of course not. I just—" Trump adjusted his sombrero again. "Should I take this off?"

"That would be advisable."

He removed the hat, hair slightly flattened underneath. The mariachi band chose that moment to start playing "La Cucaracha" without being asked.

Trump spun around. "Not now! I'll tell you when!"

They stopped abruptly, mid-note.

"Perhaps we should dance?" Sheinbaum suggested, her tone suggesting she wanted this over with as quickly as possible.

"Yes! Dancing!" Trump brightened. "I've been practicing. I'm very good. Everyone says so."

They moved to the center of the floor. The pianist—confused about whether he should play over the mariachi band—started a waltz tentatively.

Trump took Sheinbaum's hand. She was taller than he expected, or maybe he'd forgotten to wear his lifts.

"You're very tall," he said.

"I am five foot seven. You are five foot eleven, according to your official records."

"More like six foot three."

"I have eyes, Presidente Trump."

They began to dance. Trump was trying too hard, pulling her too close, moving too forcefully.

"You know," Trump said, "I have tremendous respect for Mexico. Tremendous. Some people say I don't, but they're wrong. I love Mexico."

"You called us rapists and criminals."

"I said some. Not all. Big difference."

"You threatened to make us pay for a wall."

"That was just—that was negotiating. Art of the deal. You understand business, you're a smart woman."

"I understand that you failed to make us pay for your wall."

Trump's grip tightened. "The wall is very effective. Beautiful wall. Strong."

"Parts of it fell over."

"That was the wind. Very strong wind."

Sheinbaum executed a turn with perfect technique, making Trump's clumsy leading look worse by comparison. "Presidente Trump, shall we discuss the tariffs you threatened last month?"

"The tariffs are very important. For American security."

"They are for political theater. You know this, I know this. Can we please have an honest conversation?"

"I'm being honest!"

"You threatened 25% tariffs on all Mexican goods unless we stopped migration that doesn't exist at the levels you claim."

"The numbers are very bad. Huge numbers."

"The numbers are manufactured. I have shown you the actual data multiple times."

Trump tried a dip. Sheinbaum went rigid, refusing to bend.

"You have to relax," Trump said.

"I am perfectly relaxed. You are attempting a maneuver without proper warning or technique. I am simply maintaining structural integrity."

"It's just a dip!"

"It is a physics problem you are solving incorrectly." She stepped back. "Perhaps we should try a different approach."

They resumed dancing. Trump kept stepping on her feet.

"Sorry," he muttered.

"You are leading too aggressively. Dance is about partnership, not domination."

"I'm not trying to dominate—"

"Yes, you are. You do it in negotiations, you do it in public statements, and you are doing it now on this dance floor. It is your consistent behavioral pattern."

Trump stopped moving. "Are you analyzing me?"

"I am a scientist. I analyze everything." She gestured for them to continue. "Please, lead properly. Use the frame. Maintain the connection. Anticipate your partner's movement."

"I am anticipating!"

"You are bulldozing. There is a difference."

The mariachi band, sensing tension, started playing again. Trump whipped around.

"I SAID NOT NOW!"

"Presidente Trump," Sheinbaum said calmly, "perhaps you should not have hired musicians if you did not want them to play music."

"I wanted them to play at the right moment!"

"And when is the right moment?"

"When I tell them!"

"So they are here to serve your ego, not to provide musical accompaniment."

"That's not—that's not what I—" Trump was flustered now. "Look, I was trying to be respectful! The hat, the tacos, the music—I was showing that I care about your culture!"

"You were showing that you have a superficial and stereotypical understanding of my culture." Sheinbaum's voice wasn't angry, just matter-of-fact. "Mexico is not sombreros and tacos. It is a complex nation with a sophisticated economy, rich history, and diverse population. Reducing it to tourist imagery is not respect. It is condescension."

Trump's face had gone red. "I was being nice!"

"You were being patronizing. Again, there is a difference."

They had stopped dancing entirely now. Trump was breathing hard, whether from exertion or frustration Michelle couldn't tell.

"You know what?" Trump said. "You're very difficult to work with. Very negative. I was trying to make a gesture, and you're analyzing everything to death."

"I am simply pointing out that your gesture was misguided."

"Well, maybe if you were more appreciative—"

"Of what? Of being stereotyped? Of having my country reduced to a cartoon?" Sheinbaum's composure hadn't cracked once. "Presidente Trump, I came here for a dance audition. I have danced. The dancing was mediocre. The cultural sensitivity was worse. Are we finished?"

Trump opened his mouth, closed it. "The tariffs are still on the table."

"Of course they are. You threaten tariffs the way some men threaten to leave their wives. Frequently, loudly, and never convincingly." She turned to Michelle. "Mrs. Obama, thank you for the opportunity. I believe I have seen enough."

"President Sheinbaum, I apologize for—"

"No need. This has been... illuminating." She walked toward the door, paused. "Presidente Trump, a final observation. If you want to impress a woman—any woman—learn something about who she actually is rather than who you imagine her to be. It will serve you better in diplomacy and in dancing."

She walked toward the door, then paused with her hand on the frame. "However, I will say this: you have better rhythm than I expected. With proper instruction, you might actually become competent."

Trump's head snapped up. "Really?"

"I said 'might.' Do not overinterpret." But there was the smallest hint of something in her voice—not warmth exactly, but professional respect for potential. "Mrs. Obama, we should speak later about the selection process. I have some thoughts."

After she left, Michelle watched Trump carefully. He was staring at the door with an expression she recognized—the look of a man who'd just been simultaneously insulted and complimented by someone he wanted to impress.

"She's very direct," Trump said.

"Yes."

"Very smart."

"Yes."

"Strong. Tough." He was still staring at the door. "She didn't appreciate the tacos."

"No, sir."

"But she said I had rhythm."

"She said you *might* have rhythm with proper instruction."

"That's basically a compliment." Trump picked up the sombrero, looked at it, set it back down. "Put her in the strong maybe pile."

"After all that?"

"She's honest. Brutally honest. I respect that." He pulled out his phone, started typing, then stopped. "Actually, maybe I won't post about the tariffs yet. Don't want to—I mean, it's a negotiating tactic. Strategic silence."

"Of course, sir."

"She could be good for the first dance. Professional. Dignified. Makes me look like I can work with strong women."

"That's very... strategic of you."

"I'm a very strategic person." Trump headed for the door. "Schedule a follow-up with her. Maybe without the mariachis."

After he left, Michelle sat alone with her notes. She pulled out her phone and sent a text to a number with a Mexican country code:

*President Sheinbaum, thank you for that performance. Very effective. Would like to discuss the selection process further. I have a proposal that might interest you.*

The response came quickly:

*I suspected you might. I am listening.*

Michelle smiled and added to her notes:

*Sheinbaum—strong maybe per Trump's request. Competent dancer, devastatingly honest, managed to insult him while keeping his interest. More importantly: she understands what I'm planning. The pieces are falling into place. Note: Trump's crush on her is obvious and pathetic. Also useful.*

The mariachi band's payment receipt was still on the table. Michelle filed it under "questionable campaign expenses" and moved on to her next audition.

# Chapter 20

# Dr. Anthony Fauci's Audition

Dr. Anthony Fauci arrived in a simple gray suit, no entourage, no fanfare. He shook Michelle Obama's hand warmly.

"Mrs. Obama, thank you for having me. I haven't been to the White House in quite some time."

"Dr. Fauci, I'm glad you could make it. I have to admit, I was surprised by your application."

"Oh, I've always enjoyed ballroom dancing. My wife and I used to go to lessons years ago. When I saw the announcement, I thought, why not? Might be fun."

"Fun," Michelle repeated carefully. "Yes. Let's hope so."

Trump entered, stopped when he saw Fauci. His face went through several expressions.

"You," Trump said.

"Mr. President." Fauci extended his hand. "It's been a while."

Trump shook it reluctantly. "You've got some nerve showing up here."

"I submitted an application for a dance audition. I was accepted. So here I am."

"You know what you did."

"I treated infectious disease as an infectious disease, yes."

"That's not—" Trump stopped himself. "We're here to dance, right Michelle?"

"Yes, sir. Just dancing."

"Fine. Let's dance." Trump moved to the center of the floor. Fauci followed, looking relaxed.

The pianist began a foxtrot. They assumed dance position. Fauci's frame was textbook perfect—shoulders back, arms positioned correctly, ready to follow Trump's lead.

"You know the steps?" Trump asked.

"I've been dancing for forty years, Mr. President. Shall we?"

They began to move. Fauci was immediately competent—smooth, balanced, anticipating Trump's movements with the ease of someone who'd spent decades reading signals.

"You're better than I expected," Trump admitted.

"Thank you. It's all about reading your partner and responding appropriately." Fauci smiled. "Not unlike public health communication, actually."

Trump's expression darkened. "Speaking of which—"

"Mr. President, perhaps we should focus on the dancing?"

"I just think we should clear the air about some things."

"There's nothing to clear. The pandemic happened. We responded. It's over."

"It's not over for me! You made me look bad!"

"Sir, I was providing medical guidance. That was my job."

They continued dancing, but Trump's movements were getting more aggressive.

"The masks," Trump said. "You flip-flopped on the masks."

"We adjusted recommendations based on evolving data. That's how science works."

"You said don't wear masks, then you said wear masks, then you said wear two masks—"

"Mr. President, we're dancing." Fauci's tone was patient but firm. "Perhaps we could discuss this another time?"

"No, I want to discuss it now. The lockdowns! You shut down the whole country!"

"I didn't shut down anything. I made recommendations. Governors made decisions."

"You influenced those decisions!"

"That was literally my job. I was the director of NIAID."

Trump tried a turn, yanking Fauci roughly. Fauci adjusted smoothly, maintaining his balance.

"And the six feet thing," Trump continued. "Why six feet? Did you just make that up?"

"It was based on decades of research about respiratory droplet transmission."

"But why not five feet? Or seven feet? Seems arbitrary."

"Mr. President, do you want to discuss epidemiology or do you want to dance? Because I'm happy to do either, but I can't do both simultaneously."

"I want to know why you made me look bad!"

"I didn't make you look any particular way. You made your own choices about how to communicate public health information."

They were barely dancing now, just shuffling around the floor while Trump ranted.

"The hydroxychloroquine! You said it didn't work!"

"Because it didn't work. Multiple studies confirmed this."

"I knew people who said it worked!"

"Anecdotes aren't data, Mr. President."

"You're doing it again! That condescending thing you do!"

"I'm stating facts. If facts feel condescending, that's not my problem."

Michelle made a note: *Dr. Fauci's patience is superhuman but not infinite.*

"The bleach!" Trump said suddenly.

"I never recommended bleach for anything except cleaning surfaces."

"You implied I was stupid for suggesting it!"

"Mr. President, you suggested injecting disinfectant. I didn't need to imply anything. The statement spoke for itself."

"That was taken out of context!"

"It really wasn't." Fauci executed a perfect chassé despite Trump's increasingly erratic leading. "Sir, I came here to dance. I'm a decent dancer. You're a decent dancer when you're focused. Could we please just dance?"

"Fine! We'll dance!" Trump yanked Fauci into an aggressive promenade. "But I want you to know, millions of people died because of your policies!"

Fauci stopped moving. Just stopped, mid-step, and looked at Trump with something that might have been disappointment.

"Mr. President, over a million Americans died despite everything we tried to do. I spent two years working twenty-hour days trying to save lives while being threatened, while my family was threatened, while people burned me in effigy. And you want to blame me for not doing enough while you simultaneously blamed me for doing too much."

"You undermined me at every turn!"

"I provided medical guidance. You chose to ignore it. Those were your decisions, not mine."

"You made me look bad on TV!"

"You made yourself look bad by contradicting basic public health measures during a pandemic!"

They were facing each other now, not dancing, just standing in the center of the East Room. Trump was red-faced. Fauci was calm but his voice had an edge Michelle had never heard before.

"Do you know what it's like," Fauci said quietly, "to watch people die while the person who could have saved them calls you a liar? Do you know what it's like to get death threats because you told people to wear a piece of cloth over their face?"

"I got death threats too!"

"Because you were president. I got them because I was trying to stop people from dying." Fauci took a breath. "Mr. President, I came here today because I enjoy ballroom dancing. I thought maybe enough time had passed. I thought maybe we could just have a pleasant afternoon dancing. But I see that was naive."

He stepped back, straightened his tie.

"Mrs. Obama, thank you for the opportunity. I think it's best if I leave now."

"Wait," Trump said. "We're not done."

"Yes, we are. I'm done being blamed for a pandemic I didn't cause. I'm done being attacked for trying to save lives. And I'm definitely done trying to have a normal human interaction with someone who can't let go of their grievances for thirty seconds."

"You owe me an apology!"

"For what? For being right? For doing my job? For not telling people what they wanted to hear instead of what they needed to hear?" Fauci shook his head. "I don't owe you anything, Mr. President. But you owe the American people the truth about your pandemic response. And we both know you'll never give it to them."

He walked toward the door. Trump followed.

"This is why nobody likes you, Fauci! You're arrogant! You think you're smarter than everyone!"

Fauci turned back, and for the first time, Michelle saw genuine anger on his face.

"I don't think I'm smarter than everyone. I think I'm smarter than you. About infectious disease. Which is my field. The field I've studied for fifty years. The field you know nothing about but insisted on overruling me on constantly."

"I'm the president!"

"And I'm a scientist. We each have our expertise. The difference is I stayed in my lane. You didn't."

"Get out."

"I'm already leaving." Fauci reached the door, paused. "For what it's worth, Mr. President, you're not a terrible dancer. When you focus on something other than your ego, you can actually be competent. But that happens so rarely, it's hard to tell."

After he left, Trump stood breathing hard, fists clenched.

"He's impossible," Trump said. "Absolutely impossible. Did you hear how he talked to me?"

"I heard both of you, sir."

"He thinks he's so smart."

"He is very smart, sir. He's one of the most respected immunologists in the world."

"That's not—he's not as smart as people think."

"Mr. President, you spent the entire audition relitigating COVID instead of dancing. Dr. Fauci tried multiple times to redirect you to the actual purpose of this meeting."

"Because he owes me answers!"

"He gave you answers. For two years. You didn't like them, so you ignored them, and then blamed him when things went wrong."

Trump pulled out his phone, started typing furiously:

*Just had very unpleasant encounter with Dr. Fauci (Mr. Flip-Flop!). He came to White House pretending to want to dance but really wanted to push his failed COVID policies. I set him straight! He was a disaster during the pandemic - killed millions with his bad advice! Hopefully he's learned something today!*

He showed it to Michelle. "Good?"

"That's... certainly a take on what just happened."

"He was rude to me!"

"He tried to dance with you. You spent the entire time attacking him."

"Because he deserved it!"

"Sir, Dr. Fauci is 84 years old. He came here to have a pleasant afternoon dancing. You made it impossible."

"He started it by being at the White House at all!"

Michelle closed her portfolio. "I'm going to add him to the eliminated list."

"Obviously. He's terrible. Worst audition yet."

"Actually, he was technically proficient and tried very hard to maintain professionalism despite your constant provocations."

"That's not how I remember it."

"I'm sure it isn't, sir."

After Trump left, Michelle sat alone, adding to her notes:

*Dr. Fauci—eliminated because the President cannot let go of COVID grievances long enough to complete a three-minute dance. Fauci was competent, patient, and ultimately pushed past his considerable tolerance for nonsense. His final comment about Trump being competent when focused on something other than his ego was both generous and damning. Note: Watching Trump blame Fauci for pandemic deaths while taking no responsibility for his own failures was depressing even by this administration's standards. Most importantly: Dr. Fauci said he just wanted to dance. A simple, human desire. Trump couldn't even give him that. If there's a metaphor for this entire presidency in these auditions, it might be this one.*

She picked up her phone and sent a text: *Dr. Fauci, I apologize for today. You deserved better.*

The response came a few minutes later: *Mrs. Obama, I appreciate that. But I've spent the last four years dealing with worse. Today was almost refreshing - at least he was honest about his feelings. And for what it's worth, the East Room is still beautiful. Give my regards to your husband. – Tony*

Michelle smiled sadly and put her phone away.

"You tried, Tony," she said to the empty room. "You tried."

# Chapter 21

# Russell Vought's Audition

Michelle Obama read the name on her schedule and felt a headache coming on.

"Russell Vought," she said aloud to her assistant. "Director of the Office of Management and Budget. Principal architect of Project

2025. The man currently dismantling the federal government department by department."

"He submitted an application, ma'am. Said he wanted to 'eval-
uate the ballroom project for potential cost savings.'"

"He wants to audit a dance audition?"

"Apparently."

Michelle looked at her two pencils, her full notepad, the pianist
warming up in the corner. She had a feeling some of these things
wouldn't survive the next hour.

Russell Vought entered carrying a clipboard, a calculator, and
the energy of someone who'd just found a typo in the federal
budget. He was trim, intense, wearing a suit that looked like it had
been purchased to last exactly fifteen years and not one day more.

"Mrs. Obama." He shook her hand with mechanical efficiency.
"Thank you for this opportunity."

"Mr. Vought. I understand you're here to dance?"

"Dance and assess. I believe in multitasking. The American tax-
payer deserves efficiency." He looked around the East Room with
a critical eye. "This is a large space. Are all these lights necessary?"

"We're using them."

"But ALL of them?" He pulled out his calculator. "If we reduced
lighting by thirty percent, we could save approximately—"

Trump burst in. "Russ! My favorite budget guy!" He clapped
Vought on the shoulder. "You're doing amazing things! Cutting all
that waste! The bureaucrats are terrified of you!"

"As they should be, Mr. President. Government has become
bloated and inefficient."

"That's what I keep saying! Cut, cut, cut!" Trump made chopping motions.

Vought's eyes lit up. "Actually, sir, those hand gestures use unnecessary energy. If you simply—" He demonstrated a smaller,

more economical gesture. "This achieves the same communicative goal with forty percent less movement."

Trump stared at him. "You want me to cut how I cut?"

"Efficiency in all things, sir."

Michelle made a note. Vought immediately noticed.

"Mrs. Obama, I see you have two pencils."

"Yes."

"Why two?"

"One is a backup."

"Backups are wasteful. You should use one pencil until it's completely depleted, then acquire another." He held out his hand. "I'll dispose of the redundant one."

"You want to take my pencil?"

"I want to optimize your resource allocation."

Michelle clutched both pencils. "These are my pencils."

"Taxpayer-funded pencils."

"These are MY PERSONAL PENCILS that I brought from home!"

"Oh." Vought made a note. "Still, the principle stands."

Trump was already moving to the center of the floor. "Come on, Russ! Let's dance! Show Michelle how efficient you are!"

Vought approached the dance floor, studying it like a general surveying a battlefield. "Before we begin, I have some concerns."

"About what?" Michelle asked.

"The piano." He pointed at the pianist. "Do we need live music? A recording would be more cost-effective."

"The President requested live music for all auditions."

"Wasteful." Vought made another note. "What about the dancing itself? The waltz traditionally uses a one-two-three count. Have we considered a one-two count? Eliminating thirty-three percent of the beats would save time and energy."

"That's not a waltz anymore," Michelle said. "That's just... stepping."

"Efficient stepping."

Trump was getting impatient. "Russ, can we just dance?"

"Of course, sir." They moved into position. Vought held up one hand. "Actually, Mr. President, why are we using both hands? One hand should be sufficient for leading."

"You need two hands for ballroom dancing!"

"Says who?"

"Says... ballroom dancing!"

"I'd like to see the cost-benefit analysis on that." But Vought assumed the traditional position, Trump leading.

The pianist began. They started to dance, but within seconds, Vought was analyzing.

"This step sequence seems redundant," he said. "We're essentially covering the same floor space multiple times. If we optimized the route—"

"It's dancing, not MapQuest!"

"All movement can be optimized, sir." Vought continued moving but pulled out his calculator mid-step. "By my calculations, if we eliminated every third step, we'd reduce energy expenditure by—"

"Put the calculator away!"

"But the data—"

"NO DATA WHILE DANCING!"

Vought pocketed the calculator reluctantly. They continued, but he kept muttering. "Inefficient... unnecessary twirling... this turn could be executed with half the rotation..."

Michelle watched, transfixed, as Vought attempted to audit a waltz in real-time.

"Mr. President," Vought said, "your tie is very long. Have you considered that a shorter tie would require less fabric and reduce wind resistance during turns?"

"My tie is perfect!"

"It's four inches longer than necessary for its core function."

"Its core function is looking good!"

"That's subjective and therefore unmeasurable."

They attempted a more complex pattern. Vought executed it correctly but with visible disapproval.

"This formation requires us to move in a circle," he observed. "A straight line would be more direct."

"Waltzes are CIRCULAR!"

"Wasteful." Vought was making mental notes. "Also, Mrs. Obama, I noticed you're using full sheets of paper for your notes. Have you considered using both sides?"

"I AM using both sides!"

"What about the margins? Those represent unused space."

"THE MARGINS ARE FOR MARGIN!"

"Definitionally wasteful."

Trump tried to dip Vought, but Vought resisted, remaining rigidly upright.

"Dips serve no practical purpose," Vought explained. "They're purely aesthetic and increase the risk of injury, which would raise insurance costs."

"They're ROMANTIC!"

"Romance doesn't appear in the federal budget." Vought checked his watch. "Also, we've been dancing for four minutes. The average dance is three minutes. We're thirty-three percent over time."

"BECAUSE YOU KEEP STOPPING TO CALCULATE THINGS!"

"Improper time management on both our parts."

Michelle had stopped taking notes. She was just watching in horrified fascination.

"Mr. Vought," she said, "can you just dance? Without optimizing everything?"

"I don't understand the question."

"Can you just... exist in the moment without measuring it?"

Vought thought about this. "No. That would be irrational."

The music ended. Vought immediately stepped back and began his assessment.

"Overall efficiency rating: forty-two percent. Major areas for improvement: eliminate redundant steps, reduce hand contact points from two to one, shorten tie length, optimize floor pattern, replace live music with recording, reduce lighting by thirty percent—"

"ENOUGH!" Trump said. "This isn't a budget hearing! This is dancing!"

"All activities should be evaluated for cost-effectiveness, sir."

"Not DANCING! Dancing is supposed to be fun!"

"Fun is inefficient."

Trump turned to Michelle. "He's too much. Even for me. And I LOVE cutting things!"

Vought was still consulting his notes. "If I may, Mr. President, I've also identified several cost savings opportunities in the ballroom project itself."

"Oh no," Michelle muttered.

"The ninety-thousand-square-foot design is excessive. Sixty thousand would be adequate. The crystal chandeliers could be replaced with LED fixtures at one-tenth the cost. The marble—"

"The marble is staying!"

"But economically—"

"THE MARBLE IS STAYING! THE CHANDELIERS ARE STAYING! THE WHOLE BEAUTIFUL BALLROOM IS STAYING EXACTLY AS I DESIGNED IT!"

"That's fiscally irresponsible, sir."

"I DON'T CARE!"

Vought made a note. "I'll flag this project for future review."

"You will NOT flag my ballroom!"

"It's my job to flag wasteful spending."

"Your job is to do what I say!"

"Actually, my job is to manage the federal budget in accordance with—"

"GET OUT!"

Vought blinked. "Sir?"

"Out! This audition is over! You're eliminated!"

"But we haven't completed the evaluation—"

"ELIMINATED! E-L-I-M-I-N-A-T-E-D! All the letters! No cost savings on the spelling!"

Vought gathered his clipboard and calculator. "This seems like an emotional rather than rational decision, sir."

"EVERYTHING I DO IS EMOTIONAL! THAT'S WHAT MAKES IT GREAT!"

"Emotions are unmeasurable and therefore—"

"OUT!"

After Vought left, still making notes on his clipboard, Trump stood breathing hard.

"That man sucks the joy out of everything," he said.

"He tried to take my pencil," Michelle said, still clutching both of them protectively.

"He wanted me to use one hand!"

"He suggested eliminating letters to save ink."

"He calculated my tie length!"

They looked at each other, united in their rare agreement that Russell Vought had gone too far.

"Put him in the no pile," Trump said. "The permanent no pile. The gold-plated, expensive, inefficient no pile."

"With pleasure, sir."

After Trump left, Michelle added to her notes (using both pencils, out of spite):

*Vought—eliminated because he attempted to audit a dance in real-time and suggested eliminating one-third of the waltz to save energy. He tried to confiscate my backup pencil, criticized the President's tie length, and recommended replacing the pianist with a recording. By the end, he was suggesting cost savings for the ballroom itself, which caused Trump to actually experience genuine anger about government efficiency for the first time in his life. Note: If this is the man dismantling the federal government, we're in serious trouble. He can't even let people dance without calculating the cost-per-step ratio. Most importantly: I'm keeping both my pencils. He can pry them from my cold, dead, inefficiently duplicated hands.*

She looked at her two pencils, her full notepad, the pianist still sitting at the piano.

"Thank you for not being eliminated to save costs," she told the pianist.

"Ma'am?"

"Never mind. Just... play something joyful. Something inefficient and wasteful and completely unnecessary."

The pianist played Beethoven's "Ode to Joy." Michelle closed her eyes and listened, both pencils still clutched firmly in her hands.

# Chapter 22

# Narendra Modi's Audition

Michelle Obama heard the music before she saw anyone. Not the pianist's usual classical repertoire, but something else—drums, strings, a pulsing rhythm that made the East Room's chandeliers vibrate slightly.

The doors burst open. Prime Minister Narendra Modi entered, not in a simple suit but in traditional embroidered kurta, followed by what appeared to be four backup dancers in vibrant costumes.

"Mrs. Obama!" Modi pressed his palms together and bowed. "Namaste."

"Prime Minister Modi, welcome. And... friends?"

"My dance ensemble! For the audition!" Modi gestured to the dancers, who immediately began stretching and warming up. "You said to bring what was needed for the dance, yes?"

"I meant... emotionally ready. Not an entire dance troupe."

"In India, we believe in doing things properly. With energy! With passion! With—" He snapped his fingers and the music volume increased. "—pizzazz!"

Trump entered, stopped dead. "What is happening?"

"Mr. President! Namaste!" Modi pressed his palms together again, bowing deeply.

Trump looked at Michelle. "Why is he praying at me?"

"He's greeting you, sir. Namaste is a traditional Indian greeting."

"Oh." Trump awkwardly mimicked the gesture, but kept his palms about a foot apart. "Nama... stay?"

"Namaste," Modi corrected gently. "It means 'the divine light in me bows to the divine light in you.'"

"There's light in me?"

"Metaphorically speaking."

"I knew that. Obviously." Trump looked at the backup dancers. "Who are they?"

"The ensemble! For our Bollywood dance number!"

"This is a ballroom dance audition. Like waltz. Foxtrot."

Modi laughed, a big, genuine laugh. "Mr. President, why do a simple waltz when we can do THIS!" He snapped his fingers again. The music shifted to a full Bollywood soundtrack, and the backup dancers launched into synchronized choreography.

Trump watched, transfixed and horrified, as they executed complex hip movements, arm waves, and what appeared to be a coordinated shimmy.

"I can't do that," Trump said flatly.

"Of course you can! Anyone can dance! It is in the human spirit!" Modi was already moving, demonstrating a basic Bollywood step. "See? Hip, hip, turn, arms up! Very simple!"

"That's not simple. That's—you're doing like six things at once."

"The body has many parts! Why use only the feet?" Modi grabbed Trump's hands. "Come! Join me! We will dance like Shahrukh Khan!"

"Who?"

"Bollywood superstar! Very famous! Very talented!"

The backup dancers surrounded them, creating a moving circle of color and energy. Modi tried to guide Trump through the steps.

"Hip movement!" Modi instructed. "Loose! Free! Like water flowing!"

Trump attempted to move his hips. It looked like he was trying to dislodge something uncomfortable.

"No, no! Fluid! Watch!" Modi demonstrated again, his movements smooth and practiced.

"I don't think my hips do that," Trump said.

"All hips do that! You are simply blocking your natural energy! Your chakras are misaligned!"

"My what?"

"Chakras! Energy centers! You are blocked here—" Modi pointed at Trump's midsection "—and here—" his chest "—and definitely here." His forehead.

"There's nothing wrong with my energy!"

"Your aura says otherwise." Modi was still dancing, somehow conducting this conversation while executing complex footwork. "Very orange. Very chaotic."

"Orange is a great color!"

"It is the color of the sacral chakra. Creativity, yes, but also—how do I say—unprocessed emotions."

Michelle was writing furiously: *Modi is reading Trump's aura mid-dance. This is the best audition yet.*

Trump tried to follow Modi's movements but looked like someone having a medical emergency in slow motion. The backup dancers adjusted their formation to accommodate his complete lack of rhythm.

"Arms up!" Modi called. "Like you are embracing the universe!"

Trump raised his arms stiffly.

"No! With joy! With celebration! Like this!" Modi's arms flowed upward gracefully.

Trump's arms rose like rusty gates.

"You are very tense, Mr. President. Have you considered meditation?"

"I don't have time to sit around doing nothing."

"Meditation is not nothing! It is everything! It is connecting to the divine consciousness within!"

"I connect to consciousness by tweeting."

"That is not the same."

The music shifted to a faster tempo. Modi's movements became more elaborate—spins, arm flourishes, coordinated with the backup dancers in perfect synchronization.

Trump just stood there, turning in a slow circle, arms occasionally moving in random directions.

"Mr. President," Modi said, executing a perfect turn while somehow maintaining eye contact, "in Hindu philosophy, we believe in karma. You know karma?"

"Yeah, like, what goes around comes around."

"Precisely! Your actions create consequences that return to you. Sometimes in this life, sometimes in the next."

"The next what?"

"Life. Reincarnation. The soul's eternal journey through many bodies."

"You think we get multiple lives?"

"I know we do. The Bhagavad Gita teaches us—"

"So if I screw up this life, I can fix it in the next one?"

Modi stopped dancing. "That is... not quite the message."

"But I'd get another chance, right?"

"The goal is to break the cycle, not continue making the same mistakes in perpetuity."

"Sounds like quitting to me."

Modi closed his eyes briefly, as if seeking patience from a higher power. "Let us continue dancing."

They resumed, though "dancing" was generous for what Trump was doing. Modi tried a different approach.

"Think of the dance as a conversation between souls!"

"I don't want my soul talking to people. That's weird."

"It is beautiful! It is the essence of connection!"

"I connect by making deals."

"That is transactional. Dancing is transcendent!"

"Transcendent doesn't make money."

Modi spun away, then back, his kurta flowing. "Mr. President, do you know the story of Shiva's cosmic dance?"

"Who?"

"Shiva. The destroyer and transformer. He dances the Tandava, the dance of creation and destruction. Through his dance, the universe is maintained."

"So he's like me. Creating and destroying things."

"He is a god."

"I'm practically a god. Some people say that. Very smart people."

Modi looked at Michelle. "Is he always like this?"

"Every single day," Michelle confirmed.

The backup dancers attempted to incorporate Trump into a formation, but he kept going the wrong direction and colliding with them.

"Perhaps we try something simpler," Modi suggested. "Just follow my lead. Think of nothing. Empty your mind."

"My mind is very full. The fullest. So many thoughts."

"Yes, I can see that is true." Modi took Trump's hands again. "Close your eyes."

"Why?"

"To feel the music. To connect to the rhythm of the universe."

Trump closed his eyes. Modi began a slower, gentler movement.

"Feel the energy flowing," Modi said softly. "Feel yourself as part of the great cosmic dance."

"I feel like I'm about to fall over."

"Open your eyes then."

Trump opened them. "This isn't working."

"Because you are resisting! You cannot dance while holding on to your ego!"

"My ego is tremendous! Why would I let go of it?"

"Because the ego is an illusion! The true self is—"

"My ego is NOT an illusion! It's very real! Everyone knows about my ego!"

Modi stopped, took a deep breath. "Mr. President, I have a question."

"What?"

"Why did you want to build this ballroom?"

"To have the most beautiful event space in the world."

"But why? What will it bring you that you do not already have?"

Trump opened his mouth, closed it. "It'll be tremendous."

"But will it bring you peace?"

"Peace is boring."

"Will it bring you joy?"

"Joy is for people who aren't winning."

The music swelled at that moment—a particularly infectious rhythm, drums and strings building to something irresistible. Michelle had been sitting through fifteen auditions, maintaining professional composure through dog shootings, cross-choking incidents, hypnotic eyes, and Trump mistaking world leaders for rabbis.

She looked at her notes. She looked at Trump standing stiffly, completely missing the point of everything. She looked at Modi and his dancers, moving with such pure joy, such freedom.

The music pulsed.

Michelle Obama stood up.

"Mrs. Obama?" Modi said, surprised.

She set down her portfolio, kicked off her heels, and walked to the center of the floor.

"If you're not going to dance properly," she said to Trump, "someone should."

"What are you—"

But Michelle was already moving. And not the careful, professional movements she'd maintained for eight years in the White House. Real dancing. Her hips found the rhythm immediately, her arms flowing with the music, her whole body responding to the Bollywood beat like she'd been waiting for this moment through every painful audition.

Modi's face lit up. "YES! This is dancing!"

He moved to join her, and suddenly they were partners—Modi leading with his practiced choreography, Michelle following effortlessly, both of them grinning.

The backup dancers immediately incorporated her into the formation. They'd been trained to adapt, and Michelle Obama was a much better dancer than the President of the United States.

Trump stood frozen, watching his ballroom audition judge dance with his audition candidate.

"Wait, you can dance like that?" Trump said.

Michelle executed a perfect spin. "Always could."

"But you never—when I—"

"You never asked. You just assumed." She was breathless, laughing, moving through the choreography like she'd been doing it for years.

Modi was delighted. "Mrs. Obama, you have natural talent! Have you studied Bollywood?"

"I've studied a lot of things. Including how to have actual joy." She shot a look at Trump. "Unlike some people."

The music built to a crescendo. Modi and Michelle moved in perfect synchronization, the backup dancers creating a kaleidoscope of color around them. It was everything a dance should be—joyful, free, transcendent.

Trump watched, his face cycling through confusion, jealousy, and something that might have been recognition that he'd been missing something fundamental about dancing this entire time.

The song ended. Michelle and Modi struck a final pose, breathing hard, both grinning.

The backup dancers applauded. Even the pianist, who'd been sitting idle, clapped.

Michelle walked back to her chair, slipped her heels on, picked up her portfolio like nothing had happened.

"Thank you, Prime Minister," she said, only slightly breathless. "That was... needed."

"The honor was mine, Mrs. Obama. You dance with your whole spirit."

"Unlike some people," Trump muttered.

"Yes," Modi agreed pleasantly. "Unlike some people."

Trump's face reddened. "I could have danced like that if I wanted to."

"But you didn't want to," Michelle said, making a note. "That's the difference."

"I was being professional!"

"Professional is dancing like you mean it. Not dancing like you're afraid of looking foolish."

"I'm not afraid of anything!"

"You're afraid of joy, Mr. President. I just watched you turn down an opportunity to experience pure happiness because you couldn't let go of your ego for three minutes."

Modi nodded. "This is what I tried to tell you. The ego is—"

"My ego is FINE!" Trump was getting agitated now. "And I don't need a lecture from someone who just broke protocol to dance with an audition candidate!"

"You're right," Michelle said calmly. "I did break protocol. Because watching you resist joy for the hundredth time finally broke something in me. Consider it my resignation from caring about your inability to experience human connection."

"You can't resign! You're the judge!"

"I'm still the judge. I'm just not pretending anymore that any of this is normal."

Modi watched this exchange with interest. "Mr. President, perhaps Mrs. Obama's spontaneous dancing is trying to teach you something."

"Teach me what?"

"That life is not a transaction. Dancing is not about winning. Joy is not for people who aren't winning—joy is for people who are *living*."

Trump opened and closed his mouth several times. Finally: "You both ganged up on me."

"We danced," Michelle corrected. "You watched. Those are different things."

"I want a do-over."

"No."

"I could dance like that if I tried!"

"Then try!" Modi gestured to the floor. "The music can play again! Show us!"

Trump looked at the empty dance floor, at Modi's expectant face, at Michelle's skeptical expression, at the backup dancers waiting.

"No," he said finally. "This audition is over."

"Because you lost," Michelle said.

"I didn't lose! I just—this isn't my kind of music!"

"Everything is an excuse with you."

"I'm the President! I don't need to make excuses!"

"And yet you do. Constantly."

Modi pressed his palms together. "Mr. President, thank you for this experience. It has been... revealing."

"I'm not picking you for the first dance."

"I did not expect you would. You cannot dance with someone who has seen you resist joy so completely."

"I don't resist joy!"

"You just said joy is for people who aren't winning. And then you watched Mrs. Obama experience joy and called it ganging up on you. If that is not resistance, I do not know what is."

Trump pulled out his phone, started typing furiously.

Modi turned to Michelle. "Mrs. Obama, thank you for the dance. You have a beautiful spirit."

"Thank you, Prime Minister. You reminded me of something I'd forgotten."

"What is that?"

"That sometimes you have to stop observing the chaos and just dance through it."

Modi smiled, bowed, and left with his ensemble.

After the doors closed, Michelle added to her notes:

*Modi—eliminated, though he shouldn't be. Brought full Bollywood energy, tried to teach Trump about chakras and cosmic dancing, failed completely. Trump declared joy is for losers. I broke protocol and danced with Modi instead. It was glorious. Trump watched and got jealous. Note to self: Should have been dancing this whole time. The auditions would have been much more bearable. Most importantly: Modi said Trump is "dancing with his own reflection." After watching Trump's face while I danced—the confusion, the jealousy, the complete inability to understand why someone would dance just for the joy of it—I think Modi is exactly right. Trump will never find a dance partner because he's only interested in dancing with himself.*

Trump was still standing in the middle of the room, phone in hand, trying to compose a tweet that would somehow make him the winner of this interaction.

"You made me look bad," he said finally.

"No, sir. You made yourself look bad. I just danced."

"You're supposed to be neutral!"

"I was neutral for fifteen auditions. I earned one dance."

"With my audition candidate!"

"Your rejected audition candidate. Because you can't let go of your ego long enough to feel the music."

Trump stared at his phone. Started to type. Stopped. Started again.

Finally, he just left without posting anything.

Michelle sat alone in the East Room. Her feet hurt a bit. Her hair was slightly disheveled. Her professional composure was completely shattered.

She felt wonderful.

"Thank you, Prime Minister Modi," she said to the empty room. "Namaste."

# Chapter 23

# Pam Bondi's Audition

Michelle Obama looked up from her notes and did a double take. The woman entering the East Room was unmistakably Pam Bondi—same power suit, same aggressive walk, same calculating eyes. But the hair was completely wrong.

Instead of Bondi's signature platinum blonde helmet, perfectly shellacked into submission, she had... straggly brown hair. Unkempt. Almost mousy. It looked like she'd been caught in a rainstorm and given up.

"Attorney General Bondi," Michelle said carefully. "Are you... alright?"

"I'm fine. Why?" Bondi touched her hair self-consciously. "Oh, this. Haven't you heard?"

"Heard what?"

"They just discovered that yellow dye number eighteen is a carcinogen. Class A. Very dangerous. The FDA issued an emergency bulletin last week."

"I... don't think that's true."

"Well, it should be true. Until I can get the EPA to override the decision—which I'm working on, believe me—I'm not taking any chances." Bondi patted her brown hair. "Safety first."

"The EPA doesn't regulate hair dye."

"They should. Add it to the list." Bondi pulled out a small notebook and wrote something. "Speaking of lists, I'll need yours."

"My what?"

"Your list. Of the leading audition candidates. The finalists. However you're tracking them."

Michelle's hand instinctively moved to cover her portfolio. "Why would you need that?"

"To narrow the competition, obviously." Bondi said this like it was the most reasonable thing in the world. "I can open investigations into their backgrounds. Find something prosecutable. Tax issues, campaign finance violations, jaywalking—doesn't really matter. The point is to eliminate them as viable candidates."

"You want to indict the President's other dance partner options?"

"I want to serve the President. If that means strategic prosecutions, then yes." Bondi smiled, cold and sharp. "It's what I do."

"That's... no. Absolutely not. I'm not giving you any lists."

Bondi's smile didn't waver but her eyes went flat. "Mrs. Obama, I'm the Attorney General of the United States."

"And I'm the judge of this audition. My lists are confidential."

"Nothing is confidential from the Justice Department."

"My personal notes are."

"Are they though?" Bondi made another notation. "We could discuss that. At length. In a legal setting."

"Are you threatening me?"

"I'm clarifying the scope of federal authority." Bondi's voice stayed pleasant, but there was steel underneath. "But we can table that discussion for now. Where's the President?"

Trump entered on cue. "Pam! You're here! Great! You look—" He stopped, staring at her hair. "What happened to you?"

"Hair dye concerns, sir. Yellow dye number eighteen is a potential carcinogen."

"Since when?"

"Since I decided it might be. I'm waiting for the science to catch up."

"But your hair looks terrible."

"I know, sir." Bondi touched it again, almost proudly. "But I'm willing to look terrible for you. That's loyalty."

Trump seemed genuinely moved. "That's... that's actually very loyal. Most people wouldn't sacrifice their hair for me."

"Most people don't understand what true service means, sir."

Michelle made a note: *This is somehow more disturbing than the dog shooting.*

They moved to the center of the floor. Bondi's movements were crisp, efficient, almost military. Her posture was perfect, her frame precise, but there was something cold about it—like watching a machine execute a program.

The pianist began a waltz. They started dancing, and immediately Bondi began her litany.

"Mr. President, you look very strong today. Very commanding."

"Thank you, Pam."

"Your leadership on the ballroom project has been visionary. Truly visionary."

"I think so too."

"Some people don't appreciate vision. But I do. I appreciate everything about you."

Trump was eating it up, but even he looked slightly uncomfortable with the intensity.

"Your hand placement is perfect, sir. Everything you do is perfect."

"Well, I don't know about perfect—"

"Perfect," Bondi repeated firmly. "Your decisions are always correct. Your instincts are always right. Anyone who questions you is wrong and probably criminal."

"That's a little—"

"I've already opened seventeen investigations into your critics this week. Would you like me to open more?"

Trump missed a step. "Seventeen?"

"Preliminary inquiries. Nothing formal yet. But I can escalate if you'd like."

"Based on what?"

"Based on them criticizing you, sir. That's enough."

Michelle's pen was flying: *She's not even hiding it anymore.*

They continued dancing, Bondi maintaining perfect form while simultaneously conducting what amounted to a loyalty pledge.

"Your tie is beautiful, sir."

"It's the same tie I always wear."

"But today it's especially beautiful. Everything about you is especially beautiful today."

"You're being weird, Pam."

"I'm being devoted, sir." Bondi's voice stayed level, her ice-queen affect never cracking. "There's a difference."

Trump tried a turn. Bondi executed it flawlessly while pulling out her notebook.

"Are you taking notes?" Trump asked.

"Just documenting things that might be prosecutable."

"During our dance?"

"I can multitask, sir. It's one of my best qualities. That and my willingness to abuse prosecutorial authority for your benefit."

"You shouldn't say that out loud."

"Why not? It's what you hired me for."

Trump looked at Michelle helplessly. She just shrugged.

They continued dancing, Bondi alternating between obsequious praise and casual mentions of her various investigations.

"Your posture is magnificent, sir. I've opened three grand juries today. Your rhythm is impeccable. I'm looking into the finances of that reporter who wrote the unflattering article. Your—"

"Can you stop prosecuting people for five minutes?"

"I could, but why would I? It's how I show my devotion."

"It's creepy."

"It's efficient." Bondi's brown hair flopped into her face. She pushed it back irritably. "I cannot wait to get this EPA override approved. This hair is intolerable."

"Why don't you just dye it anyway?"

"Because I need to be seen suffering for you, sir. It demonstrates my willingness to sacrifice."

"Your hair is not a sacrifice!"

"Everything is a sacrifice when it's for you, sir. My dignity, my ethics, my professional reputation—all of it. Gladly given."

Trump actually backed away slightly mid-dance. "That's... you need to dial it back, Pam."

"I don't know how to dial back, sir. I only have one setting: complete and total loyalty."

They resumed dancing, but Trump was clearly getting uncomfortable with the combination of sycophancy and casual admissions of corruption.

"What if," Bondi said, still in her pleasant, icy tone, "I prosecuted everyone else who auditioned? Then by default, you'd have to pick me."

"That's not how this works."

"Why not? It's efficient. It's strategic. It shows commitment."

"It shows insanity!"

"Those are often confused, sir."

Michelle stood up. "I think we've seen enough."

"But we haven't finished the dance!" Bondi protested, still maintaining perfect waltz form.

"You've threatened to indict your competition, admitted to abusing your prosecutorial authority, and you're dancing with terrible hair as a loyalty test. I think we're done."

Bondi released Trump and turned to Michelle with that same cold smile. "Mrs. Obama, I should mention—refusing to provide requested information to the Attorney General could be considered obstruction."

"Of what? A dance audition?"

"Of justice. I'm very flexible with definitions."

"Are you threatening to indict me?"

"I'm noting that our interaction today may merit further review."

"Pam!" Trump said. "You can't threaten Michelle!"

"Why not? She's obstructing our dance partnership."

"That's not—she's the JUDGE! She's supposed to judge!"

"Then she should judge correctly. In my favor."

"That's not how judging works!"

Bondi pulled out her notebook again. "I'm adding this conversation to my case file."

"You have a case file on this audition?"

"I have case files on everything, sir. It's called being prepared." She snapped the notebook shut. "So, am I selected for the first dance?"

"NO!" Trump and Michelle said simultaneously.

Bondi's expression didn't change. "I see. That's disappointing. And possibly prosecutable."

"You can't prosecute me for not picking you!" Trump said.

"I can investigate whether your decision-making process was influenced by foreign agents, domestic enemies, or insufficient appreciation for loyalty."

"GET OUT!"

"Yes, sir." Bondi collected her things with the same crisp efficiency she'd brought to the dance. "But I want it noted that I came here prepared to serve you completely. Hair sacrificed, ethics abandoned, prosecutorial authority weaponized—all for you. And you rejected it."

"Because it's insane!"

"Because it's honest." Bondi headed for the door, her terrible brown hair the only disheveled thing about her. At the threshold, she turned back. "Mr. President, when you do select your dance partner, please provide me with their name immediately. I'll need time to build a case."

"A case for what?"

"Whatever you need a case for. That's how loyalty works."

After she left, Trump stood breathing hard. "She threatened to indict you."

"She threatened to indict everyone," Michelle said.

"Is she always like this?"

"Yes, sir. That's why you appointed her."

"I thought she'd be less obvious about it!"

"She's many things, but subtle isn't one of them."

Trump pulled out his phone, started typing, then stopped. "If I post anything negative about her, she'll probably open an investigation into me."

"Very likely."

"That's not how this is supposed to work! I'm the President!"

"Tell that to your Attorney General."

"I can't! She'll prosecute me!"

Michelle closed her portfolio. "Welcome to the bed you made, sir."

"That's not helpful."

"Neither is appointing people based solely on their willingness to abuse power for you."

"But she has terrible hair now! That should count for something!"

"It counts as disturbing, sir. Not as loyalty."

After Trump left, Michelle added to her notes:

*Bondi—eliminated because she's willing to prosecute everyone in America if it helps her win a dance audition. Showed up with intentionally terrible hair as a "sacrifice" for Trump. Tried to get my list of candidates to indict them. Threatened to investigate me for obstruction of justice. During the dance, alternated between obsequious praise and casual admissions of corruption. Trump was actually disturbed by her, which takes real effort. Note: She has a case file on this audition. A CASE FILE. On a DANCE AUDITION. Most importantly: If this is what loyalty looks like in this administration, the country is in even more trouble than I thought.*

She looked at her portfolio, thought about Bondi's request for the list, and added a lock to her bag.

"Not taking any chances," she said to the empty room.

# Angela Merkel's Audition

Angela Merkel arrived exactly on time, wearing a sensible pantsuit in her signature color palette of "European bureaucrat." She carried a small notebook and moved with the purposeful efficiency of someone who'd spent sixteen years managing the largest economy in Europe.

"Mrs. Obama, good afternoon." Her handshake was firm, businesslike.

"Chancellor Merkel, thank you for coming."

"Former chancellor. I am retired now. But precision in titles is important, yes?"

"Yes, of course."

Merkel looked around the East Room with the evaluating gaze of someone conducting an inspection. "The acoustics are adequate. The floor is suitable for dancing. We should have no problems if everyone follows the correct procedures."

Michelle made a note: *She's going to hate this.*

Trump entered seven minutes late. Merkel glanced at her watch.

"Mr. President, you are late."

"I'm not late. I'm exactly when I need to be."

"The audition was scheduled for 2 PM. It is now 2:07. That is late."

"Seven minutes isn't late."

"Seven minutes is seven minutes. Time is not negotiable." Merkel opened her notebook, made a notation. "We begin with a handicap."

"A what?"

"In Germany, we believe punctuality reflects character. You have demonstrated poor character."

Trump's face reddened. "I have tremendous character!"

"That remains to be seen. Shall we dance?"

They moved to the center of the floor. Merkel assumed the follow position with mathematical precision—shoulders back, frame perfect, feet positioned at exactly the correct angle.

"I will lead," Trump said.

"Yes, that is traditional. Please do so correctly."

The pianist began a waltz. Trump placed his hand on Merkel's back—too low.

"Nein," Merkel said immediately. "Higher. The hand goes on the shoulder blade, not the lower back. This is basic."

"I know where my hand goes!"

"Then why is it in the wrong place?" She physically moved his hand up. "There. This is correct."

Trump's jaw tightened but he started moving. Within two steps, Merkel stopped.

"Your posture is incorrect."

"My posture is fine!"

"You are leaning forward approximately fifteen degrees. The proper waltz position requires a vertical spine with shoulders aligned over hips. Stand up straight."

"I AM straight!"

"You are demonstrably not straight. Perhaps you are unaware of your own posture?" Merkel adjusted his shoulders. "This is straight. Feel the difference."

"I can't feel any difference!"

"That is because you have poor kinesthetic awareness. We will work on this."

They resumed. Trump tried to lead into a turn.

"Nein, nein!" Merkel stopped again. "You must signal the turn before executing it. The lead is not a surprise attack."

"I didn't attack you!"

"You yanked my arm without warning. That is not leading, that is hauling."

"I was just—"

"You were being imprecise. Precision is essential. Watch." Merkel demonstrated the proper leading technique. "Feel? The subtle pressure? The gentle indication of direction? This is how you communicate with your partner."

"I communicate fine!"

"Your divorce rate suggests otherwise."

Trump's mouth opened and closed. Michelle coughed to cover a laugh.

"Can we just dance?" Trump asked through gritted teeth.

"We are attempting to dance. You are making it difficult through incorrect technique."

They started again. Trump's movements were getting more aggressive, which made Merkel's corrections more frequent.

"Your frame is collapsing."

"It is not!"

"Your left arm has dropped three centimeters. Maintain the structure."

Trump raised his arm with exaggerated force.

"Now it is too high. This is not the limbo. Find the correct height and maintain it."

"YOU'RE IMPOSSIBLE!"

"I am precise. There is a difference." Merkel consulted her notebook. "So far you have made eleven distinct errors. That is 3.7 errors per minute. This is not acceptable."

"You're counting my mistakes?"

"Of course. How else do we measure improvement?" She made another note. "Though I see no improvement yet."

Trump tried a dip. Merkel went rigid as steel.

"Absolutely not."

"Why not?"

"You have not demonstrated sufficient competence for advanced maneuvers. First master the basics, then we discuss dips."

"I can dip whoever I want!"

"Technically, yes. Successfully? No." Merkel stood firm. "Attempting a dip with your current skill level would result in injury. Probably mine. I decline."

They went back to basic steps, but Trump was fuming now, which made his dancing worse, which made Merkel's corrections more pointed.

"You are not counting the music."

"I don't need to count!"

"Everyone needs to count. The waltz is three-quarter time. One-two-three, one-two-three. You are doing something closer to one-two-thud."

"There's no thud!"

"There is definitely a thud. Listen." She demonstrated his heavy-footed stepping. "Thud-two-three, thud-two-three."

"That doesn't sound like me!"

"That sounds exactly like you. Michelle, does that sound like him?"

Michelle looked up from her notes. "I'm staying out of this."

"Wise," Merkel said. "Mr. President, we must also discuss your breathing."

"What's wrong with my breathing?"

"You are breathing through your mouth, heavily, like you have run a race. This suggests poor cardiovascular fitness. Perhaps less hamberder, yes?"

"Did you just say hamberder?"

"I believe that is how you spell it? Based on your social media?"

Trump pulled out his phone. "I'm checking that."

"We are dancing, not tweeting."

"I can multitask!"

"No, you cannot. You have demonstrated this repeatedly over the last four minutes." Merkel physically pushed his phone hand down. "Concentrate on the dancing."

"You can't tell me what to do!"

"Someone must. You clearly do not tell yourself what to do, as evidenced by your lack of discipline."

They continued in tense silence for perhaps fifteen seconds before Merkel stopped again.

"Your rhythm is inconsistent."

"MY RHYTHM IS FINE!"

"You just did four beats in a three-beat measure. That is mathematically incorrect."

"Math has nothing to do with dancing!"

"Everything has to do with math. I have a PhD in quantum chemistry. Trust me, math is everywhere."

"Well, I have a degree in business from Wharton!"

"Did you attend classes or just pay someone to write your papers?"

Trump's face went purple. "I ATTENDED CLASSES!"

"Then you received a very poor education in rhythm." Merkel made another note. "Fifteen errors now. We are trending in the wrong direction."

Michelle checked her watch. They'd been dancing for eight minutes and had covered perhaps thirty seconds of actual successful waltz.

"Perhaps we should wrap up," Michelle suggested.

"Excellent idea," Trump said quickly.

"No, we continue," Merkel said firmly. "He is making progress."

"I am?"

"No. But he could be if he listened to corrections instead of arguing with them."

"I'm not arguing, I'm defending my dancing!"

"Your dancing does not need defending. It needs improving." Merkel adjusted her frame. "Again. From the beginning. And this time, count out loud so I know you are at least attempting to find the rhythm."

"I'm not counting out loud like a child!"

"You are dancing like a child. Counting would be an improvement."

They went through another minute of Merkel's corrections punctuated by Trump's increasingly angry rebuttals.

"Posture!"

"It's FINE!"

"Frame!"

"ADEQUATE!"

"Rhythm!"

"PERFECT!"

"Timing!"

"TREMENDOUS!"

Finally, Merkel stopped, stepped back, and closed her notebook with an air of finality.

"This is not working."

"I KNOW it's not working! You keep stopping!"

"I keep stopping because you keep being wrong. And you refuse to accept correction."

"I don't need correction!"

"Mr. President, in Germany, we have a saying: 'Einsicht ist der erste Schritt zur Besserung.' Do you know what this means?"

"No."

"It means 'insight is the first step to improvement.' You have no insight into your dancing because you refuse to acknowledge your errors. Without insight, there can be no improvement. Without improvement, there can be no successful partnership."

"I have plenty of insight!"

"Name one thing you did wrong today."

Trump opened his mouth. Closed it. "You were too critical."

"That is not something you did wrong. That is you blaming me for your inadequacy."

"I'm not inadequate!"

"Your dancing is inadequate. Your posture is inadequate. Your rhythm is inadequate. Your ability to accept feedback is catastrophically inadequate." Merkel tucked her notebook into her bag. "Mrs. Obama, thank you for the opportunity, but I am afraid this is not possible."

"Wait," Trump said. "You're quitting?"

"I am recognizing reality. Another German trait you might consider adopting."

"You can't just quit!"

"I can and I am. Teaching requires a willing student. You are not willing. You are defensive, resistant, and frankly exhausting."

"I've dealt with you for four years! You're the exhausting one!"

"Yes, you 'dealt with' me by ignoring climate agreements, insulting NATO, and creating chaos at every G7 meeting. This is your standard approach—create problems, blame others, learn nothing." Merkel adjusted her sensible purse. "I am too old and too retired to endure it again."

She walked to the door, paused, turned back.

"Mr. President, one final observation. In physics, we have a principle: an object in motion stays in motion unless acted upon by an outside force. You are in motion—constant, chaotic motion. But you resist every outside force that might correct your trajectory. This is why you collide with everything."

"That's not—I don't collide—"

"You collide constantly. With facts, with allies, with basic competence. Today you collided with a waltz. Tomorrow it will be something else. But the pattern remains: motion without direction, energy without purpose."

"GET OUT!"

"I am already leaving. No need to shout. Germans have excellent hearing." She opened the door. "Auf Wiedersehen, Mr. President.

I would say it has been a pleasure, but I am German. We do not lie about such things."

After she left, Trump stood in the center of the East Room, breathing hard, fists clenched.

"Fifteen errors," he muttered. "There weren't fifteen errors. Maybe two. Three tops."

Michelle added to her notes: *Merkel—eliminated after eight minutes of trying to teach Trump basic waltz technique. She corrected his posture, frame, rhythm, timing, hand placement, and breathing. He argued with every correction. She kept a running count of his errors (fifteen in eight minutes). Her final assessment: he is "motion without direction, energy without purpose." This may be the most accurate description of his presidency ever articulated. Note: She called him out on the "hamberder" tweet. He had no comeback. Small victories.*

"She was too picky," Trump said to the empty room. "Germans are too picky. That's their problem."

He pulled out his phone and posted: *Just finished audition with Angela Merkel (Germany). Very rigid, very critical, kept stopping to make corrections instead of just DANCING! This is why Germany has so many problems—too many rules, not enough action! I danced perfectly but she wouldn't admit it. Sad!*

Michelle read it over his shoulder. "You argued with her for eight straight minutes instead of dancing."

"Because she kept interrupting!"

"To correct your mistakes."

"I DON'T MAKE MISTAKES!"

"You made fifteen in eight minutes. She counted."

Trump glared at his phone, started to type another defense, deleted it. "Put her in the no pile."

"She already eliminated herself, sir."

"Then put her in the double-no pile."

"There is no double-no pile."

"MAKE ONE!"

# THE SELECTION

# Chapter 25

# The Therapy Session

Michelle Obama lay on the sofa in their private living room, one arm draped over her eyes. She'd been home for a week, but the auditions still played on a loop in her mind—Noem's exploding face, Patel's hypnotic eyes, the dead Yorkshire terrier, Khamenei's mai tais, Trump asking Clarence Thomas if Pin Point, Georgia was near Tehran Street.

Barack sat in the armchair across from her, legal pad balanced on his knee, reading glasses perched on his nose. He'd assumed an expression of professional concern, though the corner of his mouth kept twitching.

"So," he said in his best therapist voice, "tell me about the dog."

"Which one? The one that got shot or the President?"

"Let's start with the one that got shot."

Michelle sat up slightly. "Her name was Buttons. She was a Yorkshire terrier. She weighed maybe four pounds. Kristi Noem shot her in the East Room during her audition."

Barack wrote something on his pad. "And how did that make you feel?"

"How did it—Barack, she shot a dog named Buttons!"

"But your feelings about it. We need to explore your emotional response."

"My emotional response was 'what the hell is happening in my former home.'"

"Good, good. That's progress." He made another note. "And the face situation?"

"Her face was falling apart. Literally. Extensions everywhere, lips the size of grapefruits, eyebrows migrating toward her hairline." Michelle closed her eyes. "And then she just... shot the dog. Didn't even break stride."

"Mmm-hmm. And Trump's reaction?"

"He put her in the maybe pile."

Barack's pen stopped. "I'm sorry?"

"The maybe pile. Because she was 'loyal and decisive.'"

"The woman who shot a dog during a dance audition."

"Is in the maybe pile. Yes."

Barack removed his glasses and pinched the bridge of his nose. "I'm supposed to be helping you process this, but I'm developing my own trauma."

Michelle laughed despite herself. "Welcome to my last three weeks."

"Let's try something else." Barack consulted his notes. "The Supreme Court Justice who had an existential crisis?"

"Thomas. Arrived late, Trump thought he was Khamenei—"

"Wait, what?"

"Long story. Black robes, similar expression. Trump insisted Thomas was the Iranian Supreme Leader coming back for more mai tais."

"The Iranian—" Barack stopped. "You know what? I'm not even surprised anymore. Continue."

"Thomas realized mid-waltz that he'd given immunity to someone completely undeserving. Had a full breakdown. Left his robes on a chair."

"His judicial robes?"

"Draped over a chair like he'd quit the Court on the spot."
Michelle smiled at the memory. "It was actually kind of beautiful.
A moment of moral clarity set to a waltz."

Barack made a note. "We'll call that one a win. What else?"

"The eight-year-old."

"Please tell me the eight-year-old went well."

"Little Johnny Martinez. Brought a dinosaur named Rex. Called
Trump's feet 'clown feet.' Asked better questions than most reporters. Told Trump he should dance with his own children sometime."

"And Trump's response?"

"Complete confusion. The concept had literally never occurred
to him."

Barack set down his pad. "Michelle. I'm going to ask you something as your husband, not your therapist."

"Okay."

"How are you actually doing?"

She was quiet for a moment. "I watched twenty auditions.
Twenty-one (if you count Stormy) different people trying to dance
with a man who can't dance. Can't listen. Can't let go of his ego
long enough to feel music. Can't connect with another human
being for three minutes without making it about himself."

"That sounds exhausting."

"It was. But it was also... clarifying." Michelle sat up fully now.
"I watched him reject kindness from Fauci. Wisdom from Elder
Nehemiah. Honesty from Merkel. Even joy from Modi—who
literally brought backup dancers and tried to teach him about his
chakras."

"His chakras," Barack repeated.

"Very blocked, apparently. Orange and chaotic."

"That tracks."

Michelle stood, walked to the window. "But here's the thing. I also watched him be exactly who he is. No filter, no pretense. Just pure, undiluted Trump for hours and hours. And by the end, I realized something."

"What's that?"

"I know exactly what to do."

Barack studied her. "That sounds ominous."

"It's not ominous. It's justice." She turned back to him, smiling for the first time in days. "He's building a three-hundred-million-dollar monument to his ego. And I'm going to use it against him."

"Should I be worried?"

"Only if you're on Trump's side."

"Never have been, never will be."

"Then you're fine." Michelle stretched, feeling the tension finally leaving her shoulders. "Actually, I think I'm done with therapy. I feel much better."

"That was fast."

"Turns out all I needed was to say it out loud. I know what I'm doing now."

Barack closed his legal pad. "Are you going to tell me the plan?"

"Not yet. But you'll enjoy it. Trust me."

"I always do." He stood, kissed her forehead. "For what it's worth, I'm sorry you had to sit through all that."

"Don't be. It was worth it." She headed for the door, then paused. "Oh, and Barack? Clear your schedule two weeks from Saturday. We're hosting a dinner party."

"For whom?"

"Everyone who auditioned. With spouses."

"Even the one who shot the dog?"

"Especially the one who shot the dog. And a few surprise guests."

"This plan of yours—"

"Is going to be perfect. Now if you'll excuse me, I have a phone call to make."

After she left, Barack sat alone with his notes. He flipped through the pages—dog shooting, hypnotic eyes, mai tais, clown feet, judicial robes, chakras.

"Twenty auditions," he said to the empty room. "She sat through twenty of these."

He made one final note on his pad: *Michelle is planning something. It's going to be spectacular.*

Then he went to check his tuxedo. Whatever was coming, he wanted to look good for it.

# Chapter 26

# The Lobbying Campaign

The flowers arrived on Monday.

Michelle was having coffee when the doorbell rang. A deliveryman stood on her porch holding an arrangement so large he was barely visible behind it. Roses, orchids, lilies, and several flowers Michelle couldn't identify, all in varying shades of powder blue.

"Mrs. Obama? Delivery from Senator Lindsey Graham."

She signed for them, read the card: *"To the most discerning judge in American history. Your wisdom is matched only by your beauty. The President is lucky to have you. I am lucky to know you. Forever yours in service and admiration, Lindsey Graham. P.S. I remain available for the position. P.P.S. Day or night. P.P.P.S. Seriously, any time. P.P.P.P.S. Please call."*

The flowers arrived again on Tuesday. Different arrangement, same powder blue theme, same signature. By Wednesday, Michelle had converted the guest room into a temporary greenhouse.

Thursday's bouquet came with a handwritten poem: *"Roses are red, violets are blue, The President needs a partner, that partner is true. Nobody follows quite like me, Please pick me, Michelle, pretty please."*

"He rhymed 'blue' with 'true,'" Barack observed, reading over her shoulder. "That's technically not a rhyme."

"He's desperate, not a poet."

Friday's arrangement included a small tree. Saturday brought a flowering bush that required two deliverymen. By Sunday, Michelle called Graham's office.

"Senator, this has to stop."

"The flowers? But I thought—"

"I have a rainforest in my guest room. My allergies are out of control. No more flowers."

Silence. Then: "What about a gift basket?"

"Nothing. No gifts. No contact. The decision will be made based on merit, not bribes."

"It's not a bribe, it's an expression of—" The line went dead. Michelle had hung up.


On Tuesday morning, Barack walked outside to get the newspaper and looked up. In the sky above their house, a small plane was skywriting.

He squinted at the emerging letters: **I... O-N-L-Y... H-A-V-E...**

"Michelle!" he called. "You need to see this!"

She joined him on the lawn. They watched as the message completed itself:

**I ONLY HAVE EYES FOR YOU**

"That's actually sweet," Barack said. "Who do you think—"

The plane circled and began a second message:

**- KASH PATEL, FBI DIRECTOR**

"Oh no," Michelle said.

**P.S. I AM WATCHING**

"Is that a romantic gesture or a threat?" Barack asked.

"With Patel, it's both."

The plane made a third pass:

**TRUST ME. CHOOSE ME. I SEE YOU.**

"Okay, that's definitely a threat," Michelle said.

She called the FBI.

"This is Michelle Obama. Your director is skywriting over my house."

"Yes, ma'am. We're aware. He filed it as official Bureau business."

"How is this official Bureau business?"

"He classified it as 'candidate outreach and surveillance optimization.' We're as confused as you are."

The plane was still circling. Michelle could now see Patel in the cockpit, waving.

"Can you make him stop?"

"He's the director, ma'am. We don't really tell him what to do. Mostly he tells us what to do, and we try not to make direct eye contact."

Michelle hung up. The skywriting continued for another hour:

**YOUR PORCH LIGHT IS OUT. SECURITY RISK.**
**I HAVE OPENED AN INVESTIGATION INTO THE**
**SUSPICIOUS SQUIRREL IN YOUR OAK TREE.**
**DID YOU KNOW YOUR GUTTERS NEED CLEANING?**

Wednesday brought an email from Pam Bondi's official Attorney General account. Subject line: "Campaign Materials for Your Consideration."

The attachment was a video file. Michelle almost didn't open it. Professional curiosity won.

The video opened with dramatic music—the Top Gun theme. Pam Bondi appeared in a flight suit, sitting in the cockpit of a fighter jet. Her terrible brown hair was stuffed under a helmet.

"Some people," Bondi's voice narrated, "think they deserve to dance with the President. They're wrong."

The jet roared across the sky. Bondi checked her instruments.

"As Attorney General, I don't just fight for justice. I fight for victory."

The jet approached a cluster of targets on the ground. As the camera zoomed in, Michelle recognized faces photoshopped onto cartoon bodies: Merkel, Trudeau, Modi, Fauci, Thomas, all the other candidates.

"And when you're fighting for the President," Bondi continued, "you eliminate the competition."

She pressed a button. The cargo hold opened.

Instead of missiles, an enormous payload of excrement fell from the plane, raining down on the cartoon candidates. Each target was buried under a tidal wave of CGI feces while Bondi grinned in the cockpit.

"Pam Bondi," the video concluded. "The only choice. The loyal choice. The choice that literally dumps on everyone else."

The screen faded to her official seal as Attorney General.

Michelle stared at her laptop. "She made a shit video. The actual Attorney General of the United States made a shit video."

Barack appeared behind her. "Is that—are those real people?"

"All the other candidates. She's bombing them with feces."

"And she sent this to you officially?"

"From her government email."

Barack was quiet for a moment. "You know, sometimes I miss being president. Then I see things like this and I remember why I don't."


Thursday afternoon, Michelle found Mike Pence standing on her front lawn. He wasn't doing anything, just standing there, hands clasped, that unsettling smile fixed in place.

"Mr. Vice President," Michelle called from the door. "Can I help you?"

"No, thank you. Mother and I wanted to ensure you received our letter."

"I got it."

"Excellent. We'll just wait here to discuss it."

"You don't need to wait."

"Mother insists. Proper follow-up is rule forty-seven."

Michelle looked past him. Karen Pence sat in their car, watching through binoculars.

"Is she monitoring you right now?"

"She's supervising from an appropriate distance. Rule ninety-three."

"You can't stand on my lawn all day."

"Mother packed snacks. We can wait as long as necessary." He pulled out a laminated card. "I brought my audition score sheet. I'd like to review it with you line by line."

"That's not—"

"My posture was exemplary. You gave me a seven out of ten, but Mother believes that was generous and suggested I argue for a six. I'm prepared to accept either score with grace."

It took forty minutes and two calls to Secret Service before the Pences left. As their car pulled away, Karen Pence's binoculars remained trained on the house.


Vladimir Putin's letter arrived Friday through diplomatic channels, delivered by a stone-faced Russian courier who refused to make eye contact.

The envelope was cream-colored, heavy stock, sealed with actual wax. The letter inside was typed on official Kremlin stationery:

*Mrs. Obama,*

*I do not typically involve myself in such matters, but I am told that lobbying is customary in your system. Please consider this my formal expression of interest in the dance partnership.*

*I believe Donald and I would make an excellent team. We have natural chemistry, as you observed. He follows my lead instinctively. This is rare and should be encouraged.*

*I am not saying you must select me. I am simply noting that selecting someone else would be... regrettable. For everyone involved.*

*Please give my regards to your husband. I enjoyed his company during our summits, though I found him less receptive to guidance than his successor.*

*With respect and anticipation,*
*V. Putin*

*P.S. The flowers from Senator Graham are visible from satellite. You may want to address this security concern.*

Michelle showed the letter to Barack. "Is this a lobbying effort or a threat?"

"It's Putin. It's always both."

Saturday morning brought a flood of TikTok notifications. Madison had launched a social media campaign.

Michelle watched in horrified fascination as Madison posted daily videos:

*Day 1: "Manifesting being Trump's dance partner. Like, the vibes are literally so good? I can feel it happening? Periodt."*

*Day 3: "POV: You're Michelle Obama and you're about to make the best decision of your life by picking me."*

*Day 7: "Y'all, I made a vision board. It's giving main character energy. Mrs. Obama if you see this, we should totally collab?"*

*Day 12: "Update: Still manifesting. My engagement rate is literally insane rn. That's a sign, right?"*

Each video had hundreds of thousands of views. The comments were split between "yasss queen" and "this is the death of democracy."

Sunday's mail brought a crayon drawing from Little Johnny Martinez.

Michelle unfolded it carefully. Johnny had drawn the White House in bright colors. Stick figures danced in the foreground—one clearly Trump (orange face, yellow hair), one clearly Johnny (small, holding what appeared to be Rex the dinosaur).

The message, written in careful block letters: *"DEAR MRS OBAMA. REX SAYS YOU SHOULD PICK ME. I PROMISE TO BE GOOD AND NOT CALL HIS FEET CLOWN FEET EVEN THO THEY ARE. LOVE JOHNNY. P.S. MR TRUMP STILL NEEDS TO DANCE WITH HIS KIDS."*

At the bottom, in adult handwriting: *"Mrs. Obama, please disregard. I've spoken with Johnny about appropriate lobbying channels. - Mrs. Martinez"*

And below that, in Johnny's handwriting: *"REX SAYS MOM IS WRONG."*

Michelle pinned it to her refrigerator.

Kristi Noem's package arrived Monday via private courier. The box was small, professionally wrapped, with a card that read: *"I always eliminate the competition."*

Inside, mounted on a small wooden plaque, was a taxidermied Yorkshire terrier. A brass plate read: "BUTTONS - ELIMINAT-ED."

Michelle stared at it for a full minute.

"She taxidermied the dog," she said to Barack. "The dog she shot. During the audition."

"Is that even legal?"

"I don't know, but I'm calling the Humane Society."

A second note was tucked beneath the plaque: *"Loyalty means doing whatever it takes. I've proven mine. - KN"*

Tuesday brought silence. No flowers, no skywriting, no videos, no taxidermy. Michelle was reviewing her notes when the mailman delivered a simple envelope, hand-addressed in careful script.

Inside was a single page, handwritten:

*Sister Michelle,*

*Mi no write fi lobby yuh. Mi write fi tank yuh fi di opportunity an' fi di patience yuh show all a wi. Yuh work is hard, harder dan most people know.*

*Inna Rasta, wi believe dat every trial bring wisdom, every burden bring strength. Yuh carry heavy load dese past weeks, watchin' people dance widout hearin' di music, movin' widout spirit.*

*But yuh hear di music, Michelle. Yuh have di spirit. Dat's why yuh can judge true.*

*When di time come fi choose, remember dis: di best dance partner is not di one who move di best. Is di one who help yuh partner find him own rhythm, even when him don't tink him have any.*

*JAH guide yuh steps.*

*Wid respect an' blessings,*
*Elder Ras Nehemiah Johnson*

*P.S. Di answer yuh seek is already inna yuh heart. Yuh jus' need fi*
*trust it.*

Michelle read it three times, then carefully folded it and placed it in her portfolio with her audition notes.

"Everything okay?" Barack asked.

"Yeah," Michelle said, smiling. "Everything's perfect. I know exactly what I'm doing."

She picked up her phone and dialed.

"President Sheinbaum? It's Michelle Obama. We need to talk."

# Chapter 27

# The Selection

Michelle waited until Wednesday afternoon to make the call. She'd reviewed her notes one final time, read Elder Nehemiah's letter again, and confirmed everything with President Sheinbaum. The pieces were in place.

Trump answered on the first ring.

"Michelle! You've made your decision?"

"Yes, Mr. President. I'm ready to announce the selection."

"Great! Tremendous! Who is it? Just tell me now. Is it Claudia? Please say it's Claudia."

"Mr. President, I think this warrants an in-person announcement. Can you make time this afternoon?"

Silence. Then: "You want to tell me in person? In the Oval Office?"

"If you're available."

"I'm available. I'm very available. Come at four. No, three. Actually, come now. Can you come now?"

"Four o'clock is fine, Mr. President."

"Should I have people here? Staff? Photographers?"

"I think just the two of us would be appropriate."

"Just us. Very dignified. Very classy. I'll see you at four."

He hung up before she could say goodbye.

Trump was pacing when Michelle arrived. The Resolute Desk had been cleared of everything except a single red button (Michelle didn't ask). He'd changed suits since the morning—this one had shinier buttons.

"Michelle! You're here! Right on time! Sit, sit." He gestured to the chair across from his desk, then remained standing himself, too agitated to settle.

"Mr. President, perhaps you should sit too."

"I'm fine standing. Very energized today. Very ready to hear good news." He paused mid-pace. "It is good news, right? You picked someone good? Someone beautiful and smart and—it's Claudia, isn't it? Please say it's Claudia."

Michelle opened her portfolio, removed a single sheet of paper. "After careful consideration of all twenty-one auditions—"

"Twenty-one? I thought there were twenty."

"Stormy was there with Melania, sir. It counts."

"Right, right. Continue."

"After careful consideration, I've selected the candidate who best combines technical skill, diplomatic significance, and appropriate representation of American interests."

Trump's hands were actually trembling. "And?"

"President Claudia Sheinbaum of Mexico."

The transformation was immediate. Trump's face lit up like a child on Christmas morning. He pumped his fist in the air.

"YES! I knew it! I knew you'd pick her!" He rushed around the desk, nearly hugging Michelle before stopping himself. "She's perfect! Beautiful, smart, tough—did you see how well we danced? The chemistry? Everyone saw the chemistry!"

"The chemistry was noted, sir."

"And she's a president! A real president! That makes me look very presidential!" He was pacing again, faster now. "We'll look incredible together. She's tall, I'm tall—well, I'm taller, obviously, but she's not short. And the symbolism! Dancing with Mexico! That shows I'm not racist! The press can't say I'm racist if I'm dancing with the President of Mexico!"

"That's not quite how racism works—"

"It's brilliant, Michelle. You're brilliant. This is exactly what I wanted. When do we announce?"

"I've prepared a press release. I thought we could issue it jointly—your office and mine."

"Let me see it." Trump held out his hand.

Michelle hesitated. "Perhaps we should review it together first."

"Just let me see it!"

She handed him the draft.

*********

## FOR IMMEDIATE RELEASE
## THE WHITE HOUSE Office of the First Lady (Emeritus)
## PRESIDENT TRUMP'S INAUGURAL BALLROOM
## DANCE PARTNER SELECTED

*WASHINGTON, D.C.* – Following an extensive audition process, Mrs. Michelle Obama, serving as selection committee chair, is pleased to announce that **President Claudia Sheinbaum Pardo of Mexico** has been chosen as President Donald J. Trump's partner for the first dance at the inaugural gala celebrating the opening of the new White House Grand Ballroom.

President Sheinbaum, who served as Mayor of Mexico City before her election as Mexico's first female president, brings exceptional qualifications to this historic partnership. THE BEST QUALIFICATIONS! EVERYONE SAYS SO! She demonstrated superior technical dancing ability, diplomatic grace, and IN-

CREDIBLE BEAUTY (VERY SMART TOO!) during her audition process.

"President Sheinbaum represents the kind of intelligent, accomplished partner befitting this momentous occasion," stated Mrs. Obama. "Her selection reflects NOT JUST HER QUALIFICATIONS BUT THE TREMENDOUS RELATIONSHIP between our nations and the AMAZING CHEMISTRY WE HAVE—the President and Mexico, that is, not me personally, but EVERYONE COULD SEE THE CHEMISTRY WHEN WE DANCED!"

The selection process evaluated twenty-one candidates over a period of three weeks. SOME WERE VERY GOOD, SOME WERE DISASTERS! Candidates included current and former heads of state, Supreme Court justices, SOME VERY LOYAL PEOPLE WHO I APPRECIATE VERY MUCH (LINDSEY!), and other distinguished individuals. THE 8-YEAR-OLD WAS ACTUALLY PRETTY GOOD BUT TOO SHORT!

President Sheinbaum released the following statement: "I am honored to have been selected for this important diplomatic and cultural event. I look forward to representing Mexico at what promises to be a truly spectacular evening." VERY GRACIOUS! VERY CLASSY! SHE GETS IT! MEXICO UNDERSTANDS THAT I'M THE BEST PRESIDENT THEY'VE EVER WORKED WITH!

The inaugural ballroom gala is scheduled for [DATE] and will feature THE MOST BEAUTIFUL BALLROOM EVER BUILT—90,000 SQUARE FEET, ITALIAN MARBLE, CRYSTAL CHANDELIERS FROM AUSTRIA (THE BEST CHANDELIERS!), GOLD FIXTURES THROUGHOUT. The construction cost of approximately $300 million represents A WISE INVESTMENT IN AMERICAN DIPLOMAT-

IC INFRASTRUCTURE AND ANYONE WHO SAYS OTH-
ERWISE IS FAKE NEWS!

The evening will commence with remarks from President
Trump (TREMENDOUS REMARKS! PEOPLE ARE SAYING
THEY MIGHT BE THE BEST REMARKS EVER GIVEN
AT A BALLROOM OPENING!), followed by the first dance.
THE MOST WATCHED FIRST DANCE IN HISTORY! Ad-
ditional dancing will follow, THOUGH OBVIOUSLY NOTH-
ING WILL TOP THE FIRST DANCE BECAUSE I'M THE
PRESIDENT AND CLAUDIA IS VERY TALENTED AND
BEAUTIFUL (DID I MENTION SHE'S A SCIENTIST? VERY
IMPRESSIVE! ALMOST AS SMART AS ME!)

All living former presidents and their spouses have been invit-
ed to attend. THE OBAMAS WILL BE THERE (MICHELLE
DID A GREAT JOB SELECTING, THOUGH OBVIOUSLY
I INFLUENCED THE DECISION). Other dignitaries, heads
of state, and select administration officials will also be present.
LINDSEY GRAHAM IS INVITED! AND EVERYONE ELSE
WHO AUDITIONED! EVEN THE ONES WHO WERE DIS-
ASTERS! (LOOKING AT YOU, FAUCI!)

For more information about the ballroom project and the in-
augural gala, contact the White House Press Office. OR JUST
FOLLOW ME ON TRUTH SOCIAL WHERE I POST THE
REAL NEWS!


*********


Trump looked up from the paper, beaming.

"This is perfect! You can really see where I improved it. The parts
in capitals—those are the important parts. The parts people will
remember."

"Yes, sir. Very... distinctive."

"We'll issue this immediately. Today. Right now." He was already reaching for his phone. "I'm posting about this. Everyone needs to know."

"The official release should go out first, Mr. President."

"Right, right. Official first, then my post, then maybe another post, then—do you think Claudia will post about it?"

"I believe she's preparing a statement."

"Good. That's good. This is going to be incredible, Michelle. The best first dance anyone's ever seen. Better than any royal wedding. Better than any movie. Just... the best."

He walked her to the door, still clutching the press release.

"Thank you, Michelle. Really. You made the right choice."

"I'm glad you're pleased, sir."

"Pleased? I'm thrilled! This is exactly what I wanted! Claudia Sheinbaum! President of Mexico! Dancing wth me! In my ballroom!"

After Michelle left, Trump sat at the Resolute Desk and read the press release again, smiling at his additions. He pulled out his phone and started typing, deleted it, started again.

Finally, he just pressed the button to issue the official release.

Within minutes, it was everywhere.

The internet had a field day with the ALL CAPS SECTIONS. Political commentators tried to parse which parts Michelle had written and which parts were Trump. Mexico's official response was polite and brief. Claudia Sheinbaum's statement was gracious and gave away nothing.

Trump spent the evening retweeting praise and arguing with critics about whether the ballroom's $300 million price tag was reasonable.

Michelle spent the evening on the phone with the remaining pieces of her plan.

Everything was falling into place.

# Chapter 28

# The Dinner Party

Michelle Obama stood in her doorway and watched world leaders, Supreme Court justices, a Supreme Leader, and an eight-year-old with a toy dinosaur arrive at her home.

"This is either brilliant or insane," Barack murmured beside her.

"It's both. That's the point."

Angela Merkel arrived first, precisely on time, carrying a bottle of German Riesling and a look that suggested she was prepared for anything. "Mrs. Obama. Mr. President. Thank you for the invitation."

"Chancellor Merkel, welcome. Please, make yourself comfortable."

Merkel surveyed the arriving guests with her evaluating gaze. "This is quite the guest list."

"That's one way to put it."

Vladimir Putin arrived without fanfare, flanked by security who took positions outside. He shook Barack's hand with that calculating grip, nodded to Michelle, and immediately gravitated toward the bar.

Narendra Modi entered with considerably more energy, his traditional kurta embroidered in gold. He pressed his palms together.

"Namaste! What a wonderful gathering! So much potential energy in one room!"

"Try to keep it contained," Michelle said.

Justin Trudeau arrived looking effortlessly perfect, as always. Melania Trump arrived separately, fifteen minutes later, saw Trudeau across the room, and chose a seat with a clear sightline. She wasn't smiling, but something in her posture suggested interest.

Mike and Karen Pence entered together—Mike in a conservative suit, Karen carrying her laminated rule cards. They surveyed the room, identified the safest corner, and claimed it immediately.

"Is that alcohol being served?" Karen asked.

"Yes, Mrs. Pence."

"Rule sixty-three prohibits Michael from being within fifteen feet of open bar service."

"We'll make a note of that."

Dr. Fauci arrived, gracious and diplomatic, immediately engaging with Merkel about European healthcare systems. Clarence Thomas came alone, without his robes, looking smaller somehow. Lindsey Graham arrived in yet another powder blue tuxedo, gravitating immediately toward anyone who might acknowledge him.

Little Johnny Martinez burst through the door, his mother apologizing behind him. "Mrs. Obama! This is SO COOL! Is that a real Supreme Court Justice? Can I meet him? Rex wants to meet him!"

"Johnny, inside voice."

"This IS my inside voice!" But he lowered it slightly, clutching Rex the dinosaur.

Madison arrived filming herself. "OMG you guys, I'm literally at Michelle Obama's house? With like, actual world leaders? The aesthetic is giving very much political thriller, you know?"

"Phone away during dinner, please," Michelle said.

"But my followers—"

"Away."

Madison pouted but complied.

Elder Nehemiah Johnson entered last, moving with that un-hurried grace, wearing simple white linen. He pressed his palms together, bowed slightly to Michelle and Barack.

"Elder Johnson, welcome."

"Blessings, sister. Blessings, brother." He looked around the room, smiled. "Interesting energy here tonight. Very interesting."

And then, just as Michelle was about to close the door, one more car pulled up. Supreme Leader Ali Khamenei emerged, his black robes flowing, two security personnel flanking him. He approached the door with the dignity of someone who'd spent decades as Iran's highest authority.

"Mrs. Obama. Thank you for the invitation." He glanced at the bar visible through the doorway. "I trust you have—"

"Mai tais. Yes. We're prepared."

"Excellent."


Dinner was served buffet-style—Michelle had figured out that assigned seating with this group would be impossible. People grav-itated toward unexpected combinations.

Little Johnny somehow ended up standing next to Khamenei at the appetizer table. He stared up at the Supreme Leader's black turban.

"Are you a wizard?" Johnny asked.

Khamenei looked down at the small boy. "No. I am a religious leader."

"What's the difference?"

"Wizards are fictional."

"Oh." Johnny considered this. "Rex says your hat is cool."

Khamenei examined the plastic dinosaur. "Rex has good taste. This is a traditional turban, worn by Islamic scholars for centuries."

"Can I try it on?"

"Absolutely not."

"That's what my mom says about her jewelry." Johnny held up Rex. "This is Rex. He's a T-Rex. He's very wise."

"I see." Khamenei accepted a mai tai from a passing server. "And what wisdom does Rex offer?"

"Mostly he says people should listen more and talk less. Also, he thinks your beard is impressive."

"Tell Rex I appreciate his discernment." Khamenei took a sip of his drink. "Your president thought I was a rabbi."

"Mr. Trump? He thinks a lot of weird stuff. One time he said windmills cause cancer."

"Did he." Khamenei smiled slightly. "Perhaps we have more in common than I thought."

Across the room, Angela Merkel found herself in conversation with Dr. Fauci.

"The pandemic response was challenging everywhere," Merkel said, "but watching it unfold here was particularly difficult."

"Watching it from inside was worse," Fauci said quietly. "Every press conference felt like negotiating with a toddler who had nuclear codes."

"We had our own challenges in Germany, but at least our toddlers understood basic epidemiology."

"I envy you that."

They stood in companionable silence for a moment, two people who'd spent their careers dealing with facts meeting a man who treated them as optional.

Vladimir Putin stood by the bar, nursing vodka, when Narendra Modi approached.

"President Putin. Enjoying the evening?"

"It is... unusual." Putin's English was careful, measured. "You enjoyed your audition, I noticed."

"Dancing should be joyful. Though President Trump seemed resistant to the concept."

"Americans are often resistant to concepts." Putin glanced at Barack across the room. "Some more than others."

"You danced with President Trump quite... intimately."

"The tango requires closeness."

"That was more than closeness. That was dominance."

Putin's expression didn't change, but something flickered in his eyes. "Perhaps you observed correctly."

"And yet he thinks he led."

"Of course he does. That is the point."

Modi tilted his head. "In Hindu philosophy, we believe the greatest power is making others feel powerful while controlling their every move."

"In Russia, we call that Tuesday."


Madison had cornered Melania Trump near the dessert table.

"Mrs. Trump? Can I just say, like, your whole vibe is literally iconic? The way you just exist while everyone else is losing it? That's giving main character energy."

Melania's expression remained neutral. "Tank you."

"And like, the way you showed up to watch Prime Minister Trudeau's audition? Everyone noticed. That was a power move."

"I don't know vhat you mean."

"Sure, sure. Totally." Madison lowered her voice conspiratorially. "But like, between us? He's literally so much better looking than—" She glanced toward where Trump would be if he were invited. "—you know."

"I know." Melania's lips curved microscopically. "Everyone knows."

Across the room, Justin Trudeau was engaged in conversation with Clarence Thomas, but his eyes tracked Melania with practiced subtlety.

Lindsey Graham had positioned himself near Elder Nehemiah, hoping proximity to wisdom might grant him relevance.

"Elder Johnson, wasn't it? I just wanted to say, your audition was very... spiritual. Very moving."

"Tank yuh, Senator."

"Though of course, the President needs someone more practical. Someone who understands Washington. Someone loyal."

"Di President have plenty loyalty around him. What him need is truth."

"Truth is important, certainly, but loyalty—"

"Senator." Nehemiah's voice was gentle but firm. "How long yuh been followin' people who don't see yuh?"

Graham blinked. "I don't—what do you mean?"

"How long yuh been givin' devotion to people who take an' take an' never give back? Who use yuh loyalty like tissue—use it once, throw it away?"

"The President appreciates—"

"Di President appreciate what yuh do fi him inna di moment. Tomorrow, him forget yuh name." Nehemiah placed a hand on Graham's shoulder. "Yuh have value, bredrin. But not di value yuh keep offerin'."

Graham opened his mouth, closed it, and walked away quickly.

Mike Pence stood rigidly in his corner while Karen monitored the room with her laminated cards. Dr. Fauci, in an act of either courage or masochism, approached them.

"Vice President Pence. Mrs. Pence. Lovely evening."

"Dr. Fauci." Pence's smile was fixed. "Mother and I were just discussing whether this gathering violates rule seventy-two."

"What's rule seventy-two?"

Karen consulted her cards. "Attending social events where more than three people disagree with our worldview."

"That must make most events difficult," Fauci observed.

"We manage through rigorous adherence to the other rules."

Khamenei drifted past, mai tai in hand, and paused. "Excuse me. You are the one with the many rules?"

"Uh, yes," Pence said. "And you are...?"

"Supreme Leader of Iran."

"Oh. Oh my." Pence's hand went to his reinforced collar. "Mother, this is—"

"I know who he is, Michael."

Khamenei studied them with interest. "I understand you also have strict religious codes governing behavior."

"We follow God's will as interpreted through careful study and Mother's guidance."

"Mother?" Khamenei glanced at Karen.

"His wife," Fauci clarified. "He calls her Mother."

"Interesting." Khamenei took a sip of his drink. "In Iran, we also have strict codes. Though we do not laminate them."

"The lamination is for durability," Karen explained. "Rules should last."

"Indeed. Though I find that rigid rules sometimes break when pressure is applied. Flexibility has its place."

"We don't believe in flexibility," Pence said. "We believe in structure."

"I believed that too, once." Khamenei's eyes were distant. "Then I danced with your president while drunk on American cocktails and questioned everything."

He moved away, leaving the Pences frozen in confused silence.

Dinner was winding down when Barack caught the musicians' eyes and gave a subtle nod. They'd been playing soft background jazz, but now they shifted to a waltz—the same waltz that had played during so many auditions.

The effect was immediate. Every person in the room who'd auditioned recognized it. Merkel's shoulders stiffened. Modi started swaying slightly. Graham looked like he might cry. Even Putin's expression changed—something that might have been amusement.

"Oh no," Fauci said.

"Oh yes," Michelle replied from across the room.

Little Johnny started doing the box step, counting out loud. "One-two-three, one-two-three!"

Modi couldn't help himself—he began to move, just slightly, his natural rhythm asserting itself. Merkel watched with her precise, evaluating gaze.

"We are not dancing," Karen Pence said firmly.

"I wasn't going to suggest it," Pence replied quickly.

Trudeau stood, extended his hand to Melania. "Mrs. Trump? Since we're among friends?"

Melania considered for exactly three seconds, then took his hand. They moved to the center of the room with practiced elegance. Everyone watched—some with appreciation, some with envy, Lindsey Graham with what looked like physical pain.

Barack leaned over to Michelle. "That was cruel."

"That was necessary. They needed to remember."

Merkel approached them. "Mrs. Obama, you are a skilled manipulator."

"I prefer 'strategic thinker.'"

"They are the same thing. I approve." She glanced at the dancing couple. "Tomorrow will be interesting, yes?"

"Tomorrow will be many things."

"I look forward to it."


The evening was ending when the doorbell rang. Michelle checked her watch—exactly on time.

She opened the door. Bill and Hillary Clinton stood on the porch, Bill with his easy smile, Hillary in a elegant pantsuit.

"Mr. President. Secretary Clinton. Thank you for coming."

The reaction inside was immediate. Conversations stopped. People turned. Even Trudeau and Melania paused mid-dance.

"Bill! Hillary!" Barack greeted them warmly, embracing both. "Glad you could make it."

The audition candidates looked at each other, confused. Why were the Clintons here? They hadn't auditioned. They weren't part of this.

Only three people in the room, besides the Clintons, knew why: Michelle, Barack, and Claudia Sheinbaum, who'd arrived late and stayed quiet in the corner, watching everything with those intelligent, evaluating eyes.

Sheinbaum caught Michelle's gaze across the room. Michelle gave the smallest nod.

Everything was ready.


Guests began to leave around ten. Little Johnny had fallen asleep on the couch, Rex clutched in his hand. Modi embraced everyone goodbye with genuine warmth. Merkel shook hands with her typical efficiency. Putin left without fanfare. Trudeau escorted Melania to her car—they talked for several minutes on the sidewalk.

Khamenei was one of the last to leave. He approached Michelle at the door.

"Thank you for the mai tais."

"You're welcome, Supreme Leader."

"And for inviting me. I did not expect to be included."

"Everyone deserved to be here tonight."

"Even though I am your enemy?"

Michelle smiled. "Tonight, you were just another person who had to dance with Donald Trump. That transcends geopolitics."

Khamenei laughed—a genuine sound. "Perhaps there is hope for diplomacy after all. Tomorrow should be very entertaining."

"I certainly hope so."

After the last guest left, Michelle, Barack, Bill, and Hillary sat in the living room. Claudia Sheinbaum had stayed behind.

"Everyone clear on tomorrow?" Michelle asked.

"Crystal clear," Hillary said. "Though I have to ask—are you sure about this?"

"Completely sure."

"He's going to lose his mind."

"I'm counting on it."

Barack looked at his wife with admiration and something like awe. "You've been planning this since the first audition, haven't you?"

"Since before the first audition. Since the moment he announced that ballroom. Since every petty, vindictive thing he's done since he's been in Washington." Michelle smiled. "Tomorrow, it all comes together."

Claudia raised her glass. "To poetic justice."

"To poetic justice," they echoed.

Outside, Little Johnny's mother was loading him into their car when he stirred awake.

"Mom?"

"Yes, honey?"

"Rex says tomorrow is going to be really important."

"Rex is very smart."

"He also says Mrs. Obama is planning something big."

His mother smiled. "Rex is very smart indeed."

Johnny clutched his dinosaur and fell back asleep, dreaming of ballrooms and dancing and a woman who knew exactly what she was doing.

# Chapter 29
# The Big Gala Opening

The White House Grand Ballroom was everything Donald Trump had promised and more. Ninety thousand square feet of Italian marble stretched beneath Austrian crystal chandeliers that cast prismatic light across walls adorned with gold leaf so thick it had required three separate applications. The ceiling soared forty feet overhead, painted with a mural depicting—and no one was quite sure who'd authorized this—Donald Trump shaking hands with various allegorical figures representing Prosperity, Victory, and what appeared to be Miss Universe 2013.

"It's giving very much Versailles," Madison whispered to her phone, filming discreetly despite Michelle's earlier warnings. "But like, if Versailles had a Gold's Gym membership, you know?"

A junior Congresswoman approached her nervously. "Excuse me, are you Madison? From the audition?"

Madison's face lit up. "OMG yes! You saw my TikToks?"

"Everyone saw your TikToks. The manifesting series? Iconic. Can I get a selfie?"

"Obviously!" Madison posed, making sure her good side faced the camera. "Tag me, okay? My engagement rate is literally insane right now."

Across the room, Little Johnny Martinez was surrounded by a group of Senate aides, all trying to shake his hand.

"You really told him his feet looked like clown feet?" one asked, awe in his voice.

"Rex told him," Johnny corrected, holding up the plastic dinosaur. "I just translated."

"That took guts, kid."

"Not really. Rex does all the hard work."

A tech billionaire from Silicon Valley crouched down to Johnny's level. "Your question about the three hundred million dollars funding schools for kids instead—that went viral in our Slack channels. We've been talking about it for weeks."

"Rex says you should do something about it then, not just talk."

The billionaire blinked. "Rex is right. Can I get a picture with him? With both of you?"

Angela Merkel stood near one of the marble columns, and she'd been approached four times in the last ten minutes by foreign diplomats wanting to discuss her audition.

"Chancellor Merkel," the French ambassador said, "is it true you counted his mistakes in real-time?"

"Fifteen errors in eight minutes," Merkel confirmed. "I kept a running tally."

"Magnificent. Simply magnificent."

A British MP joined them. "The way you corrected his posture while maintaining that expression of professional disdain—it was a masterclass in diplomatic restraint."

"It was a waltz, not diplomacy."

"In this administration, they are the same thing."

Dr. Fauci found himself cornered by three senators who wanted to hear about his audition.

"How did you not lose your temper?" one asked.

"Practice. Two years of practice."

"And he really brought up hydroxychloroquine during the dance?"

"And bleach. And the six-foot rule. And masks. He managed to relitigate the entire pandemic while attempting a foxtrot."

"That's actually impressive."

"In the worst possible way, yes."

Narendra Modi was holding court with a group that included two cabinet secretaries and the Japanese ambassador. All of them wanted to hear about his Bollywood audition.

"The backup dancers were a nice touch," the ambassador said.

"Dancing should be joyful! I brought the joy!"

"And Mrs. Obama actually joined you on the dance floor?"

Modi's face lit up. "She has natural talent! Beautiful spirit! She understood what the President could not—that dancing is about surrender, not control."

"I heard she kicked off her heels," a cabinet secretary said with obvious delight.

"The moment the music moved her soul, yes! It was glorious!"

Vladimir Putin stood alone near the bar, but he wasn't being ignored—people simply watched him from a safe distance, whispering. A brave junior diplomat from Estonia finally approached.

"President Putin, if I may—your audition with President Trump. The tango."

Putin's expression didn't change. "What about it?"

"You... you led him. The entire time. Even when he thought he was leading."

"Did I?"

"Everyone saw it. It was... it was brilliant. Terrifying, but brilliant."

Putin took a sip of his vodka. "Perhaps you observed correctly."

The diplomat retreated quickly, already texting his colleagues: *I just talked to Putin about dominating Trump through dance. My life is complete.*

Supreme Leader Ali Khamenei was an interesting case. People gave him a wide berth—he was, after all, the Supreme Leader of Iran—but they also couldn't stop staring. He stood near the bar with his second mai tai, looking surprisingly relaxed.

A State Department official gathered courage and approached. "Supreme Leader, may I ask—the mai tais. At the White House. During your audition."

"What about them?"

"It's just... unexpected. The image of you with a cocktail during an audition to dance with President Trump has become somewhat iconic in diplomatic circles."

"Life is full of unexpected moments. One must adapt." Khamenei took a sip. "These are quite good, by the way. The bartender uses the correct ratio."

Elder Nehemiah Johnson had drawn the quietest but most intense crowd. People approached him differently—not seeking gossip or selfies, but something else. Wisdom, perhaps. Clarity.

A congressman sat beside him. "Elder Johnson, I saw footage of your audition. What you said about Trump chasing things that can't fill him up—it's been haunting me."

"Why it haunt yuh, bredrin?"

"Because I do the same thing. Different things, but same emptiness."

Nehemiah nodded slowly. "First step is seein' it. Second step is choosin' different."

"What's the third step?"

"Dere is no third step. Yuh jus' keep choosin', every day, fi di rest a yuh life."

Justin Trudeau was mobbed. Between being the former Prime Minister of Canada and being objectively attractive, his audition had generated enormous interest—particularly the part where Melania had shown up to watch and clearly enjoyed Trump's humiliation.

"Is it true she smiled?" a staffer asked breathlessly.

"I couldn't possibly comment on Mrs. Trump's expressions."

"But she did come to watch your audition specifically?"

"She attended, yes."

"And you made President Trump look bad just by being competent?"

"I simply danced. If that made anyone look bad by comparison, that's not my fault."

Across the room, Melania Trump stood alone, which was how she preferred it. But people watched her too, whispering about the Trudeau audition, about her obvious satisfaction at her husband's discomfort, about the subtext that had become text.

Mike and Karen Pence had stationed themselves near a wall, as far from the open bar as rule sixty-three allowed. But even they attracted attention.

"Is it true your wife brought laminated rule cards to your audition?" a reporter asked, somehow having gotten inside.

"Mother believes in structure," Pence said with his fixed smile.

"And that you couldn't dance closer than thirty-six inches?"

"The guidelines are very clear on appropriate male-to-male physical contact."

The reporter blinked. "But you're both men. Dancing is supposed to—never mind."

Lindsey Graham worked the room with desperate energy, but now people approached him for different reasons.

"Senator Graham," a lobbyist said, "is it true you sent flowers to Mrs. Obama? For weeks?"

"I was expressing appreciation for her service—"

"Daily flower arrangements. Including a tree."

"I wanted to be thorough."

"And you wrote a poem? That rhymed 'blue' with 'true'?"

Graham's face reddened. "Poetry is subjective."

"That's not poetry, that's a cry for help."

Clarence Thomas stood alone, without his robes, and people gave him space—but not because they feared him. Because they pitied him. Word had spread about his existential crisis mid-waltz, about removing his robes and leaving them on a chair, about his moment of moral clarity while dancing with a man he'd given immunity to.

A law clerk approached carefully. "Justice Thomas, I just wanted to say—what you did during your audition. The honesty about the immunity decision. That took courage."

Thomas looked at him for a long moment. "It wasn't courage. It was recognition. There's a difference."

"Still. It mattered."

Kristi Noem was avoided. When she entered, conversations stopped, people moved away, creating a bubble of empty space around her. Everyone knew about Buttons. Everyone had seen the taxidermied evidence. She seemed unbothered, standing alone in her power, face freshly Botoxed, extensions intact, ready to shoot anything that threatened her evening.

"Is that her?" someone whispered.

"The one who shot the dog during the audition."

"And sent the corpse to Mrs. Obama."

"Jesus."

"Don't make eye contact. Just don't."

Bill Clinton surveyed the room, watching the audition candidates hold court like celebrities, watching the power players of

Washington treat them like characters in a shared cultural moment.

"Three hundred million dollars just to be humiliated in front of the world," he said quietly to Michelle.

"He did this to himself," Michelle replied.

Barack smiled. "You've thought of everything."

"I've had a lot of time to think."


At precisely eight o'clock, the lights dimmed. A spotlight illuminated a raised platform at the far end of the ballroom. Donald Trump stood there in a custom tuxedo that had reportedly required six fittings and still didn't quite fit. His hair was swept into its signature configuration, his tie was too long, his expression was triumphant.

The room fell silent.

"Ladies and gentlemen," Trump began, and his voice boomed through speakers that had cost more than most people's houses, "welcome to the most beautiful, the most spectacular, the most incredible ballroom in the history of the world!"

Polite applause. Graham's applause was not polite—it was desperate, thunderous, echoing long after everyone else had stopped.

"People said it couldn't be done. They said, 'Sir, you can't build a ballroom this beautiful. It's impossible. It's too expensive. It's too ambitious.' But I did it anyway, because that's what I do. I make the impossible possible. I make the beautiful more beautiful. I make America greater than it's ever been before!"

He paused for applause. It came, mostly from confusion about whether the speech was over.

"This ballroom—my ballroom, really, let's be honest—represents everything great about this country. The marble? Italian. The chandeliers? Austrian. The gold? The best gold. From everywhere.

The best countries, the best materials, the best craftsmanship. Nobody builds like me. Nobody even comes close."

In the crowd, a German industrialist leaned toward his wife. "He does know the marble and gold came from other countries, yes? That this is the opposite of America First?"

"I don't think he's considered that."

"Ninety thousand square feet!" Trump continued, gesturing broadly. "That's bigger than most people's houses. Bigger than most buildings! And every single square foot is perfect. People are saying it's the eighth wonder of the world. Some people are saying ninth, but I think eighth is more accurate."

Modi whispered to Nehemiah: "Does he understand that the wonders of the world are naturally occurring?"

"Him don't understand plenty things, bredrin."

"This ballroom cost three hundred million dollars. Three hundred million! Some people said that's too much. But you know what I say? You can't put a price on beauty. You can't put a price on greatness. You can't put a price on making America the envy of every nation on Earth!"

Little Johnny tugged his mother's sleeve. "Mom, Rex says three hundred million could build like a thousand schools."

"Rex is very smart, honey. And very good at math."

"And you know what the best part is?" Trump was building now, his voice rising. "Tonight, in this magnificent ballroom, we're going to witness history. The first dance. My first dance. With the perfect partner. The best partner. A partner I personally selected—well, Michelle Obama selected her, but I approved it, so really I selected her—and she's perfect!"

The crowd shifted, anticipating.

"President Claudia Sheinbaum of Mexico! Beautiful, smart, tough—everything you want in a dance partner! And she's a president! That's important! It shows I can work with other countries!

It shows I'm not—what do they call it—not racist! You can't be racist if you're dancing with the President of Mexico!"

Michelle closed her eyes briefly.

"So without further ado—and believe me, I could talk for hours about this ballroom, I have so many things to say, incredible things, but I know you're all eager to see the first dance—I'd like to invite President Claudia Sheinbaum to join me!"

Trump extended his hand toward the entrance with a flourish.

The Marine Band began a waltz.

The spotlight swung to the doorway.

No one appeared.

Trump held his pose, arm outstretched, smile fixed. "President Sheinbaum? Claudia?"

Silence.

"She's probably just—she's probably nervous. It's a big moment. Biggest moment of her life, probably. Claudia?"

Michelle Obama stepped into the spotlight. She walked across the marble floor with measured grace, carrying a microphone.

"Mr. President, if I may?"

Trump's arm dropped. "Michelle? What are you—where's Claudia?"

"I'm afraid President Sheinbaum sends her deepest apologies. She was called back to Mexico this afternoon. Urgent matters of state."

The crowd murmured. Trump's face cycled through several colors.

"What? No. No, that's not—we had an agreement! She was selected! She can't just not show up!"

"Unfortunately, running a country sometimes requires unexpected schedule changes. I'm sure you understand."

"I don't understand! This is my night! My ballroom! My first dance! You can't—she can't—" Trump was sputtering now, his carefully constructed evening collapsing in real time.

"However," Michelle continued, her voice carrying through the speakers with perfect clarity, "we do have a replacement. Someone who was gracious enough to step in at the last moment. Someone with extensive dance experience, diplomatic credentials, and"—she paused, and something that might have been a smile flickered across her face—"a personal history with the President."

Trump's eyes narrowed. "Who?"

From the entrance, Bill Clinton appeared. He was smiling, relaxed, walking with that easy Arkansas charm. And on his arm, in an elegant white pantsuit that somehow managed to be both appropriate and defiant, was Hillary Clinton.

The room erupted. Gasps, laughter quickly stifled, shocked exclamations from every corner. Little Johnny stood on his chair to see better. Putin's expression didn't change, but he raised his vodka glass in what might have been a toast. Khamenei's laugh was heard across the entire ballroom. Modi clapped his hands together in delight. Merkel's smile was small but deeply satisfied. Even Elder Nehemiah nodded his approval.

"Oh my god," Madison whispered to her phone, "this is literally the most iconic thing I've ever witnessed, periodt."

Michelle spoke into the microphone, her voice steady: "May I present former President Bill Clinton and former Secretary of State Hillary Clinton. Secretary Clinton has graciously agreed to serve as your dance partner this evening."

Bill walked Hillary to the center of the floor, to the exact spot where Trump stood frozen. He squeezed her hand, smiled at her with obvious pride, and stepped back.

Hillary looked at Trump. Trump looked at Hillary. The entire world—because cameras were broadcasting this to every news network, every streaming service, every phone on Earth—watched.

Hillary extended her hand.

"Mr. President," she said, her voice clear and strong and carrying just the faintest hint of something that might have been satisfaction or might have been justice or might have been both, "it looks like we have the first dance."

Trump's mouth opened. Closed. Opened again. No sound came out.

The Marine Band continued playing. The waltz filled the ballroom, echoing off all that gold, all that marble, all that desperate, gaudy excess.

The cameras focused on Trump's face—the realization, the horror, the understanding that he was trapped in his own monument, surrounded by witnesses, unable to refuse without humiliating himself more than he was already being humiliated.

His hand moved to his mouth, a gesture of pure, childlike shock. The world's cameras caught it, preserved it, would replay it endlessly.

Hillary's hand remained extended. Waiting. Steady.

And in the back of the ballroom, Michelle Obama stood with her husband, watching Donald Trump begin to reach out, begin to accept what was about to happen—dancing with Hillary Clinton in a three-hundred-million-dollar room he'd built to glorify himself, at an event broadcast to hundreds of millions, in a moment he'd orchestrated as his triumph that had become his perfect, poetic humiliation.

Barack leaned close. "That was cold."

"That was justice."

"What's the difference?"

Michelle smiled, really smiled, for the first time in months. "Nothing. Absolutely nothing."

The music played on.

And somewhere in that ballroom, a small boy held up a plastic dinosaur and whispered: "Rex says this is the best thing that's ever happened."

His mother didn't disagree.

# Also by Barry Robbins

6-3 and 5-4
NO! a response to donald j. trump
HELL NO! a response to donald j. trump
American Monsters
Tariff Schmariff
Trump in Windsorland
Voices of the Civil War

# About the Author

B arry Robbins writes books. Quirky books. Books with imagination, with creativity. He can do that because he's retired and is good at writing quirky, imaginative books, like this one. He's written seven political satires that won three gold medal awards. Well, no one's perfect. Upon returning from living 12 years in Finland, where he sharpened his imagination pretending he was on a sunny beach in January, he moved his attention to books of storytelling. One gold medal so far. He now resides in Florida and seldom imagines snow-covered sidewalks.

www.ingramcontent.com/pod-product-compliance
Lightning Source LLC
Chambersburg PA
CBHW051952150726
47999CB00004B/1353